Let's Hide the Word

Gloria Gaither
AND
Shirley Dobson

Joyful Ways to Build Biblical Principles into Your Home

Illustrated by RUSS FLINT

WORD PUBLISHING

Dallas • London • Vancouver • Melbourne

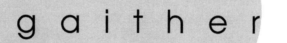

gloria gaither & shirley

Let's hide THE WORD

dobson

pictures by russ flint

WORD PUBLISHING
Dallas • London • Vancouver • Melbourne

Unless otherwise indicated, all Scripture quotations
are from the New Century Version of the Bible,
copyright © 1987, 1988, 1991, Word Publishing.
Scripture quotations marked KJV are from the King
James Version of the Bible.

Those marked NKJV are from The New King James
Version, copyright© 1979, 1980, 1982, Thomas
Nelson, Inc., Publisher.

Those marked NIV are from The Holy Bible: New
International Version, copyright © 1973, 1978, 1984
by the New York International Bible Society, used
by permission of Zondervan Bible Publishers.
Scripture quotations marked TLB are from The
Living Bible, copyright © 1971 by Tyndale House
Publishers, Wheaton, Illinois. Used by permission.

Library of Congress Cataloging-in-Publication Data
Gaither, Gloria.
    Let's hide the Word / Gloria Gaither and Shirley Dobson ;
    illustrations and book design by Russ Flint.
        p.   cm.
    ISBN O-8499-3516-4
    1. Christian life—Biblical teaching. 2. Christian education of
children. 3. Bible crafts. I. Dobson, Shirley. 1937- .
II. Flint, Russ. III. Title.
BS680. C47G35 1994
249—dc20   94-268855
                                                  CIP

table of contents

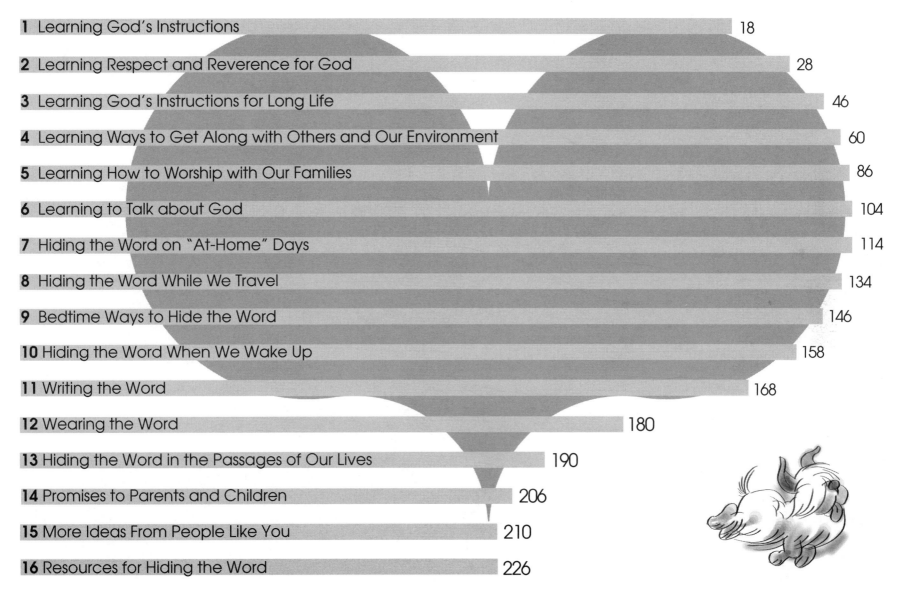

tell it to your children

Tell it to your children and your children's children;

Stamp it on the doors of their hearts.

Make it the theme of the song that you sing,

And sing it to them right from the start.

Tell it in the morning; tell it at night;

Make it your life, your joy and delight

Tell it to your children and your children's children;

Jesus must be Lord of their lives.

Tell it to your children and your children's children,

Stamp it on the doors of their hearts.

Fill up their minds with the things of the Lord,

And from them they will never depart.

Tell it with your laughter, tell it with your talk;

Tell it when you're working and tell it when you walk.

Tell it to your children and your children's children;

Jesus must be Lord of their lives.

Jesus must be Lord of their lives.

"THY WORD HAVE I HID IN MY HEART, THAT I MIGHT NOT SIN AGAINST THEE."

Live the way the Lord your God has commanded you
so that you may live and have what is good and have a long life in the land you will take. You, your children,
and your grandchildren must respect the Lord your God as long as you live. Obey all his rules and commands
I give you so that you will live a long time. Listen, Israel, carefully obey these laws. Then all will go well for you, and
you will become a great nation in a fertile land, just as the Lord, the God of your ancestors, has promised you.
Listen, people of Israel. The Lord our God is the only Lord.
Love the Lord your God with all your
heart,
all your soul, and all your strength. Always remember these commands I give you today. Teach them to your
children and talk about them when you sit at home and walk along the road. When you lie down
and when you get up. Write them down and tie them on your hands as a sign.
Tie them on your forehead to remind you,
write them on your doors
and gates.

Deuteronomy 5: 33, 6: 2–9

*M*y thanks to my parents, the late Lee and Dorothy Sickal, who early on gave me a love for the Scriptures and daily lived out their truths in our home; to my sister, Evelyn, who, because she shared the same heritage, believed in the value of this project and gave me encouragement all along the way; to Megan English, who contributed, with the great enthusiasm of a child, many creative ideas; and to my own precious family, who is daily reinforcing my conviction that God's Word is a "lamp unto our feet and a light unto our path," even in the moral labyrinth of this century's closing days. My gratitude, also, to my assistant, Deborah Tufts, who shares my passion for words and the Word.

Gloria Gaither

I'd like to express my gratitude to my mother, Alma Kubishta, who knew she needed divine assistance in raising her two children. She sent us to Sunday School and Christian camps where we learned the Scriptures and found an anchor for our lives. At a time when difficult circumstances were swirling around us, we were held steady by the eternal truths of God's word. That is why I wanted to write this book with Gloria Gaither. Today's children, living in a time of moral freefall, need that same foundation in the Scriptures. As the Psalmist wrote, "Thy word have I hid in mine heart, that I might not sin against thee" (Ps. 119:11 KJV).

I also want to thank my friend, Pat Verbal, for her creativity and the hours of research she invested in this writing project. She was joined in this effort by my assistant, Debi Westlund, who has become my "right arm" in handling day-by-day responsibilities.

Finally, I appreciate my husband, who consistently lives out God's word in public and in private. His suggestions and opinions are reflected throughout my portion of this book.

Thank you, Jim, for your unwavering love.

Shirley Dobson

I was bounding through our old Michigan farmhouse on my way out to the orchard to eat "snow apples" and feel the summer breeze in my hair when I caught a glimpse of my daddy sitting in the corner of the living room where he often sat by the window. I made an abrupt turn to run to him before going outside. He wasn't "studying" at the table where he usually prepared his sermons but just sitting in his big, green, overstuffed chair. Over his right hand was draped this big "soggy" Bible, the kind of Bible preachers have, the kind I always wanted because it fell open and hung down limp on each side when held in one hand. Now my little eyes focused on Daddy's face. Tears were streaming down his tanned cheeks, but he wasn't sad. He scooped me up in his other arm and lifted me onto his lap, still holding the Scriptures in his right hand. I didn't need to ask. I knew why Daddy was weeping. Often I had seen him deeply moved by some beautiful or awesome revelation from the Holy Spirit while he was reading God's Word. These insights and illuminations were often the topics of our discussions at the supper table and the texts read for our nightly family worship time.

What has remained with me over the years of that memory was that my father wasn't reading the Bible to prepare a sermon or a Sunday school lesson. He wasn't reading to be a "good example" to me. I had just happened in on him spending time with Jesus and listening to God speak through His Word. God had spoken and I had entered a sanctuary; in my father's embrace I, too, sensed that we were on holy ground.

My parents made the Word a very practical part of our daily lives. In fact, it is impossible for me to think of life in tidy compartments labeled "sacred" or "secular," for all of life was sacred and the Scripture was very relevant to our "secular" Monday through Friday life.

I don't remember ever being required to memorize Scripture except in Vacation Bible School during two weeks every July at the little community church where my parents pastored. But somehow, by the time I left for college, huge portions of Scripture had been entered in my memory bank and had become a part of the very fiber of my being.

When I became an adult and a young parent, I found myself wondering exactly *how* I had come to know and love the Scripture and when I was taught its meaning. I realized that my parents had taken seriously God's instructions to families from the ancient writings of Deuteronomy. Without my really noticing, they had made Scripture a part of our lives because it was a way of life for them. They had, first of all, taken God's Word into their own hearts, making it not something they *read* or even something they *did*, but something they *were*. And because the Word was in their hearts, they had "talked about it" walking, sleeping, waking, sitting—in the house, in the church, by the way, and at the table.

Every passage of our lives bore the stamp of God's Word: birthings, dyings, marryings, comings of age, departings, returnings, and remainings all were solemnized with appropriate blessings and instructions from God's Word. In season, out of season, when it was convenient, when it was difficult, when we were sufficient, inefficient, self-sufficient, or insufficient, we read the Bible together or someone was sure to quote it.

The truth and certainty of the Bible has been for me a plumb line, a measuring stick, and a compass in a crumbling culture where there are no moral absolutes. I have come to believe that equipping our families with the truth of the living Word is not an option, an opinion, or a persuasion. It is a life-and-death necessity if our children and we, ourselves, as their mentors, are to survive the disintegration of all we hold dear as the very foundations of religion turn to powder under our feet.

Morality, integrity, industry, compassion, commitment, self-discipline, hope, tranquility, honesty, faithfulness, and dependability have never been instilled in human beings by the culture or strong public opinion or governmental policy. These enduring qualities are a result of parents and other significant adults teaching truths to children, verbally and by example. When children become mature enough—if the groundwork has been laid at home—they will realize these qualities are impossible aspirations without the empowerment of a transcendent God who alone can implement our highest human ideals

Through the ages the Bible has been cherished and condemned. It has engendered devotion and denunciation. It has been ridiculed, banned, and burned. It has been dismissed and ignored. It has been embraced and treasured. Some have gone to their graves cursing and trying to abolish it; many more have died defending it. Scholars have been martyred for translating it for the common person to read. Kings have tried to make it the exclusive property of the aristocracy.

Voltaire proclaimed two and a quarter centuries ago that there would "not be a Bible on the earth except one that was looked upon by an antiquarian curiosity seeker." British bishops once called it "that damnable book." Tyndale had to flee to Germany to translate it into English, only to see the six thousand copies that were smuggled back into England seized and burned. Tyndale was eventually captured and strangled, then burned at the stake. Cromwell ordered a copy of the English Bible made available in every English church, yet under Queen Mary I, printing of the Bible was punishable by death. Queen Elizabeth called it "the jewel I love best" yet persecuted Roman Catholic scholars who then fled to the Continent and there translated the Rheims-Douay version.

But in spite of everything, the Bible has endured. Translations and paraphrases have made God's Word accessible to more men, women, and children than ever before in history. Despite Voltaire's grim prediction, more new copies are printed, sold, and read every year all over the world than ever before in history.

But the copies that are dearest to me are the ones I see nightly in my grown children's hands as they seek in its pages guidance for their young families and their own uncertain days.

As I finish this manuscript, I do not shake with fear; nor am I depressed by pessimism. I believe in the power of the Word of God, and I know that Isaiah's prophecy is true to the end of time: "The grass withers, the flower fades, but the word of God stands forever" (Isa. 40:7 NKJV).

...my little eyes focused on Daddy's face. Tears were streaming down his cheeks...

Shirley

Shortly after the collapse of communism in the former Soviet Union and the fall of the Berlin Wall, my husband received a visit from a Moscow sociologist named Mikhail Matskovsky. Dr. Matskovsky was responsible for family-related research and other scientific investigations in his country. He had come to the United States, and then to Focus on the Family, for a very specific purpose.

After a brief introduction and greeting Dr. Matskovsky said to my husband, "Let me tell you why I'm here. I want to talk to you about your belief system. I am an atheist, and I certainly do not understand your concept of Jesus Christ. We Russians must admit, however, that our 'god' died with the disintegration of communism. Now we are attempting to find a new way of thinking that will be good for our society. I have come to seek your help in identifying what might be called 'ultimate values.' Do you think the Ten Commandments would be a good place to start?"

My husband and the former Soviet official spent an hour talking about the truth of Scripture, and they have continued to work together to this day. It was interesting and encouraging to note that this social scientist recognized, even in the absence of a meaningful faith, that there was inspired wisdom to be found in the ancient Scriptures. I wish every American scientist and bureaucrat had the same appreciation for the Bible!

My own journey into the Word began when I was only eight years old. My mother sent my brother and me to a neighborhood evangelical church where I learned from a compassionate Sunday school teacher, Mrs. Baldwin, and from a Bible-teaching pastor, Reverend Penner, that God loved me and every member of the human family. Furthermore, I began to see in Scripture that God had told us how He wanted us to behave and why it was important to live by those principles.

With the encouragement of Mrs. Baldwin I memorized the Ten Commandments and began to see how they applied to my life. I understood that the Lord did not want me to lie or steal or be jealous of those who had more than we did. I saw the importance of putting God first in my life and letting Him guide my path. Ultimately, this understanding of Scripture led me to give my heart to Jesus Christ as my Lord and Savior. *That* was the pivotal moment in my entire life and has influenced everything occurring from that early experience to the present.

A few years later, this personal relationship with the Lord and the Scripture principles I had learned held me securely as my family began to disintegrate. I had an anchor in the midst of the storm. It also held me steady during the turmoil of my adolescent years, when my friends and associates began to participate in immoral and destructive activities. I was exposed to the same temptations, of course, but ringing in my ears were those familiar Scripture verses I had stored away in my heart. For example, I knew God was riding in the car with me when I was on a date, and I understood that He loved me. He wanted the best for me and had given His commandments to protect me from my own sinful desires. It was not fear of my mother's punishment or displeasure that kept me on the straight and narrow. It was respect for those biblical truths I had learned from Mrs. Baldwin and my pastor that made me want to do what was right. How unfortunate it is that many of today's children have no knowledge of what Dr. Matskovsky called "ultimate values."

A recent Gallup Poll revealed that only 3 percent of young people could name all ten of the commandments, and 15 percent could identify a mere one of them! As shocking as that revelation is, it should not surprise us. We have not bothered to teach these basic understandings of right and wrong to the next generation. In one of the most regrettable judicial decisions ever rendered, the United States Supreme Court ruled in 1980 that the state of Kentucky could not even post the Ten Commandments on the walls of its schools. Is it any wonder that so many teenagers today seem to be guided by no internal compass? Some can kill with no sense of remorse. Many become involved with sex and drugs while they're still in high school. Indeed, we appear to be approaching the period in human history Paul described in 2 Timothy 3:2–5:

> People will be lovers of themselves, lovers of money, boastful, proud, abusive, disobedient to their parents, ungrateful, unholy, without love, unforgiving, slanderous, without self-control, brutal, not lovers of the good, treacherous, rash, conceited, lovers of pleasure rather than lovers of God—having a form of godliness but

denying its power. Have nothing to do with them. (NIV)

This description of a wicked and perverse generation is remarkably relevant to our day. The culture in which we live is threatening even the children from Christian families because of the pervasive influence of peer pressure. How can we guide our boys and girls through a social environment in which the only standard of right and wrong is public opinion? Rock stars now have more influence on the behavior and beliefs of young people than do ministers or parents. To millions of teenagers physical attractiveness is far more significant than the content of one's character. As the professional tennis star, Andre Agassi, said in his television commercial, "Image is everything!" Agassi is wrong. Image is *not* everything. The immutable truths of God's Word must be the standard for our values and beliefs. Everything else is "hay and stubble."

To repeat the question many Christian parents are asking today, how can we shepherd our kids through the mine field of wickedness laid down by Hollywood and the secular media? There is only one secure answer: We must expose our children to the wisdom of Scripture from their earliest experiences. We cannot afford to be casual about that most important of assignments. Moses described the proper approach to this spiritual training when he wrote, "These commandments that I give you today are to be upon your hearts. Impress them on your children. Talk about them when you sit at home and when you walk along the road, when you lie down and when you get up. Tie them as symbols on your hands and bind them on

...my friends and associates began to participate in immoral and destructive activities.

your foreheads. Write them on the doorframes of your houses and on your gates" (Deut. 6:6–9 NIV).

I wish every boy and girl today could come under the influence of a godly person like Mrs. Baldwin, who loved the Word more than her own life. Perhaps there is such a saint in the church to which you take your children. It would be unwise, however, to depend on someone else to handle this assignment. *You*, as a mother or father, are charged with the responsibility of training up your children in the way they should go. That may be the most important task you will be given in your lifetime. No other accomplishments and no other success will compensate for failure to teach these eternal truths to the generation now around our knees.

My husband's grandmother used to gather her six children around her for daily devotions. Her prayer made such an impression on Jim's dad that he referred to it throughout his life. She prayed, "Lord, it is my most urgent request that each of these children will come to know You personally. If one of them fails to make that commitment, it would have been better that I had never been born." This is the priority she gave to her spiritual responsibility.

I encourage each of you to help your children hide the Word in their hearts. That is why we have written this book to assist in that critical task. It will be worth whatever inconvenience and effort required to convey spiritual truths to your kids while they are young and pliable. As we know so well, nothing invested in a child is ever lost.

It is my prayer that the Lord will use the ideas we have provided here to help you instill "ultimate values" and eternal truths in the hearts and minds of your chilren.

...but ringing in my ears were those familiar Scripture verses I had stored away in my heart.

"Teach them to your children, And talk about them

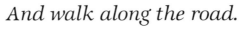

When you sit at home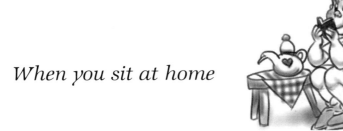

And walk along the road.

When you lie down

And when you get up.

Write them down

And tie them on your hands as a sign.

Tie them on your forehead to remind you

And write them on your doors

And gates."

Deuteronomy 6:7–8

Live the way the LORD your God
has commanded
so that you may live and have
what is good.

Deuteronomy 5:33

Since God created us, it stands to reason that He knows best how we should operate for maximum joy, effectiveness, health, peace, and harmony. He also knows the things that might cause us to self-destruct.

God's Word is like an "operations manual" for human beings. If we read the manual and do what it says, we will have the best results in our inner beings—in our souls—and in our relationship with each other and with our Maker.

In this section you will find some of the instructions God has given and some fun ways to remember them and make them a part of your life.

Section **1**

learning God's instructions

The Ten Commandments Song

Read Exodus 20:1-17.

Sing the following song to the tune of "Do-Re-Mi" from *The Sound of Music*.

One, don't worship other gods.
Two, no graven images.
Three, don't take God's name in vain.
Four, the Sabbath is for rest.
Five, respect your family.
Six, don't ever, ever, kill.
Seven, be faithful to your spouse.
And don't steal, don't lie, don't wish for others' things.

Sing other Bible passages to tunes your family knows and loves. This is a great way to memorize important verses.

Discussion questions:

1 What do other gods look like? Young children can draw a picture.

2 What are some modern-day gods? Look at the morning newspaper together for reports of misplaced priorities.

3 How is faith in God revealed in respect for the family?

The Perfect Ten

Words and Music by
Kathie Hill
and Janet McMahan-Wilson

1 a growth chart for the heart

- Using a sheet of poster board, make a Growth Chart for the Heart, labeling the sections:

  * Ask God's Guidance
  * Recognize and Avoid Sin
  * Help Someone
  * Memorize Scripture
  * Follow Jesus Example
  * Feel Thankful.

- Hang the chart on your bedroom wall.

  Make an entry in the appropriate section each time you remember to do one of the things on your chart and write down a corresponding Bible verse.

GROWTH CHART FOR THE HEART

ASK GODS GUIDANCE | RECOGNIZE AND AVOID SIN | HELP SOMEONE | MEMORIZE SCRIPTURE | FOLLOW JESUS EXAMPLE | FEEL THANKFUL

2

Next, stretch a strip of rolled shelf paper vertically on your bedroom or bathroom wall from the floor to duplicate your height. Divide the strip into several equal sections, perhaps one or two inches per section. Each time you record an entry on your chart, color in a section of your measuring strip with a marker or crayon. You might like to use a different color for each section on your chart.

Weight and height measure our physical growth. Years of school measure our educational growth. But how do we know if we are growing spiritually? God's Word says we will grow spiritually by obeying God's instructions and loving one another.

Marking a chart should not make us proud of ourselves, but rather thankful for God's grace in our lives. To get started, memorize these verses, then record them in the "Memorize Scripture" column of your chart and color in three sections on your measuring strip:

* *"See that you go on growing in the Lord."* (Col. 2:7 TLB).
* *"And Jesus increased in wisdom and stature, and in favor with God and man"* (Luke 2:52 NKJV).
* *"Grow in the grace and knowledge of our Lord and Savior Jesus Christ. Glory be to him now and forever!"* (2 Pet. 3:18).

When our bodies are attacked by germs or a virus, we can tell by the symptoms we have: a higher temperature, various aches and pains, a tired feeling, chills, coughs, a runny nose, and other discomforts. Sometimes we can be vaccinated against these illnesses so we don't have to endure the suffering they cause.

When our communities are sick, there are symptoms too: fear, violence, a sense of aloneness or isolation, disrespect for others' rights or property, betrayal, and broken promises and commitments.

The Ten Commandments were given by God to "vaccinate" communities against the attack of social illnesses that can "destroy" our families and our relationships in the community.

As a minister at New York City's Riverside Church put it, "The Ten Commandments are *not* the Ten Suggestions." If everyone were committed to God's moral absolutes, we could all live without fear of being robbed, lied to or about, cheated, violated, or betrayed. Doors could be left open, friends could be depended on, and homes would be stable.

This sense of safe community can be a reality—in our families, at least. It begins with each one of us taking seriously God's yardstick for the basics of our behavior.

TEN COMMANDMENTS
building community

2

Read the words of Jesus in Matthew 5:21–48, and John 15:12, which tell us the real "cure" for broken commandments: Love one another. Talk about how thoughts and attitudes always come before actions. How can we, as human beings, "fix" our hearts and minds so that our actions never hurt others and ourselves?

1

Study together the Ten Commandments in Exodus 20:1–17. Focus on one each week and talk about what it means and how each person in the family can live it out on a daily basis. Memorize each commandment.

3

What does Jesus say we must do immediately (before each day ends) if we do fail to be loving and thoughtful? See Matthew 5:23–24 and Ephesians 4:26.

A Child's Heart Is a Garden

The best way to hide the living Word of God in your child's heart is to keep it ever before your own eyes. We must live the Word through faith—uncompromised—and believe our faith works. What we *are* speaks louder than our words.

A child's heart is a garden. The seeds we actively and lovingly plant in our children's hearts will grow. God is able to bring them to a full harvest rising above the junk seeds of the world. As we plant God's Word, He will watch over it to perform it.

"They will be like a well-watered garden." (Jer. 31:12 NIV).

—*Jan Gee, Scotch Plains, New Jersey*

jumbled instructions

You will need:
- strips of paper
- a pen or pencil
- a large package of alphabet macaroni
- a roll of double-sided tape
- 5" x 7" index cards in bright colors
- felt-tip markers

1

Write on each strip of paper one instruction from God's Word about how we should live our lives. Include the Bible reference.

2

Put the strips in a small basket.

3

Divide the macaroni equally into small paper cups so each person in the family has some.

4

Give each person a 5" x 7" colored card and enough double-sided tape to make a stripe across the card.

5

At the signal to start, each person chooses a strip of paper from the basket and then spells out the "instruction" by arranging the macaroni letters on the double-sided tape.

When everyone is finished, take turns reading the instructions aloud. The macaroni letters can be secured by covering them with a strip of regular tape. Cards can be decorated with markers to illustrate the instructions and displayed and used for memory work.

draw a commandment

1 Have a poster contest to see who can come up with a creative way to illustrate one of God's commandments. Set a time when the posters must be entered.

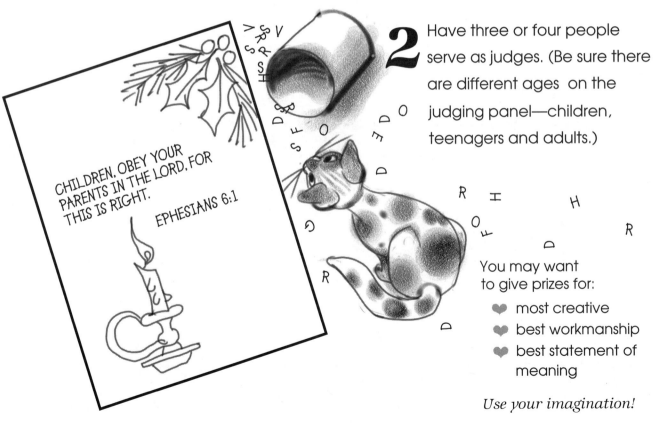

2 Have three or four people serve as judges. (Be sure there are different ages on the judging panel—children, teenagers and adults.)

You may want to give prizes for:

- ♥ most creative
- ♥ best workmanship
- ♥ best statement of meaning

Use your imagination!

3 Display the finished posters in a large room or in your backyard.

4 Send invitations to the "gallery showing." (Be sure to include time, place, date, and time the winners will be announced.)

5 When the guests arrive, invite them to enjoy refreshments and browse through the gallery, paying close attention to workmanship, symbolism, creativity, and content.

6 When the judges have decided, have everyone sit down for the awarding of prizes.

1 From an 8 1/2" x 11" sheet of construction paper cut ten strips lengthwise of equal width.

2 Write one of the Ten Commandments from Exodus 20 on each strip.

3 Make a circle of the First Commandment strip by gluing or taping the ends together.

4 Link the next commandment strip through the first and glue or tape it.

5 Continue until all ten are linked together to form a chain.

6 Hang the chain on your bedpost or from a peg on the wall of your room.

7 As you find other commandments of God, add links to your chain. Notice how the strength of the chain depends on the strength of each link, just as the strength of our moral character depends on our keeping each of God's commandments.

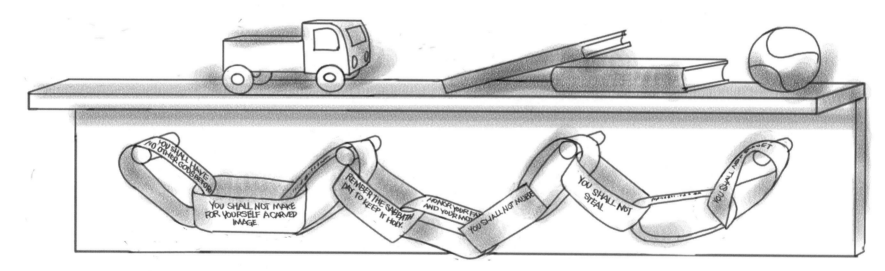

commandment chain

teachable moments

Each Child's Uniqueness

As a single mother I have found that my two children are uniquely different. God has told me to give the Word to them in different ways. My eleven-year-old daughter enjoys church and has long talks with me and her godmother, who is a blessing. My little boy wakes up saying, "Hallelujah!" Our prayer time together is much more lively.

—*Camille E. Allen, Washington, D.C.*

You, your children, and
your grandchildren
must respect the LORD
your God
as long as you live.

Deuteronomy 6:2

God is our Father. He is also our best friend. He loves us more than we can ever comprehend. He loves us even before we please Him; He loves us when we disobey.

He is an awesome God. He has such incredible power that just by speaking the original Word into empty space He caused everything that is in the whole galaxy and all other galaxies to come into existence. One word from His mouth made the sky, the oceans, all the plants and animals, mountains, rivers, insects, and finally, us!

So He deserves our respect. Without Him we wouldn't even BE! This respect is more than just a choice. It is necessary to make our lives work right. God must be the "bottom line" to everything we do, the beginning and ending of everything we care about. Before anything else existed, there was God. When everything stops existing, there will be God.

To keep our lives in order, then, respect for God is very important. In this section we will share some ways to live with a respect for God.

Section 2

the Bible: a library of literature

The Bible is a collection of books, letters, and prophetic literature. It is more fun to read if you know what kind of book you're reading, who wrote it, and why it was written. The Bible is divided into two major parts:

The Old Testament: the books written before Jesus came

The New Testament: the books written after Jesus came

All of time is divided that way too. Dates before Christ's birth are B.C. These years progress backward, with the highest numbers being the longest time ago. For example, dates 412 years before Jesus was born would be written 412 B.C. while 824 A.D. would describe the dates 824 years after His birth.

Testament means "covenant," or "agreement," so the *Old Testament* simply means God's "*old covenant*" with His people on how they should live under the law.

New Testament means God's "new covenant," or how people should live now that they know Jesus.

The Old Testament has five kinds of books in it:

- ♥ **Law books**
- ♥ **History books**
- ♥ **Poetry collections**
- ♥ **Major prophets** (books by men who wrote what God told them would happen in the future on a broad scale)
- ♥ **Minor prophets** (books by lesser-known men about thefuture of fewer people or a shorter span of time) The New Testament also has five kinds of books:
- ♥ Gospels (the real truth about what Jesus did and said while He was here on earth)

- ♥ **History** (an accurate account of what happened to the new believers after Jesus left to go to His Father)
- ♥ **Paul's letters** (letters Paul wrote to encourage and teach the new believers as they spread out all over the world)
- ♥ **General letters** (letters written by other believers to encourage and inform each other of what God was doing)
- ♥ **Prophecy** (the very last book of the Bible, which tells what was going to happen from the time the church was established until the end of time)

the Bible library

Duplicate this drawing and put it in your Bible to help you learn and remember the kind of book you are reading whenever you read the Bible.

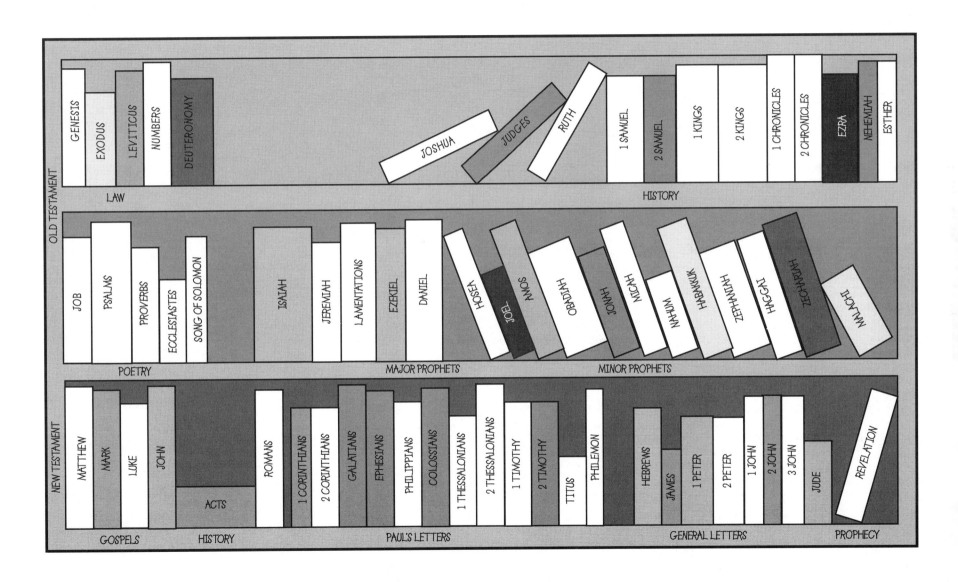

Books of the Old Testament

1. Let us sing the books of Mo - ses, of Mo - ses, of

Mo - ses. Let us sing the books of Mo - ses, for he wrote the

(2nd time only)

law. First, Gen - e - sis; sec - ond, Ex - o - dus; Third Le - vi - ti - cus; Fourth

D.S. (2nd time only)

Num - bers; And the fifth is Deu - ter - on - o - my, The last of them all.

Verse 2:
Let us sing the books of Hist'ry, of Hist'ry,
of Hist'ry.
Let us sing the books of Hist'ry, Which tell
of the Jews.
There's Joshua, and Judges, And the story
of Ruth,
Then First and Second Samuel, And First and
Second Kings.
Then First and Second Chronicles, Which give
us the Records,
Then Ezra, Nehemiah, And Esther, the queen.

Verse 3:
Let us sing the books of Poetry, of Poetry,
of Poetry,
Let us sing the books of Poetry, The songs
the Jews sang.
Job the patient, Psalms of David, The Proverbs
of a wise one;
And then Ecclesiastes, And the Song of Solomon.

Verse 4:
Let us sing the Major Prophets, Major Prophets,
Major Prophets,
Let us sing the Major Prophets, The greatest of
them all.
Isaiah, Jeremiah, Who wrote Lamentations;
Then Ezekiel and Daniel, Who were true to
their God.

Verse 5:
Let us sing the Minor Prophets, Minor Prophets,
Minor Prophets,
Let us sing the Minor Prophets, There are twelve
of them all.
Hosea, Joel, Amos, Obadiah, Jonah, Micah, Nahum,
Habakkuk,
Zephaniah, Haggai, Zechariah, Malachi.

Books of the New Testament

Mat - thew, Mark, Luke, John, Acts and E - pis - tle to the Ro - mans,

First and Sec - ond Cor - in - thi - ans, Gal - a - tians and E - phe - sians; Phil-

ip - pi - ans, Col - os - sians, First and Sec - ond Thes - sa - lo - ni - ans,
He - brews, James, _____ First and Sec - ond Pet - er,

First and Sec - ond Tim - o - thy, Ti - tus and Phi - le - mon.
First, Sec - ond, Third John, Jude and Rev - e - la - tion.

Bible scramble

Using a colored marker label two 3 x 5 cards "Old Testament" and "New Testament." Next, using a different-colored marker, label other 3 x 5 cards with the names of the divisions of the Bible: Law, History, Poetry, Major Prophets, Minor Prophets, Gospels, History, Paul's Letters, General Letters, New Testament Prophecy. Use a third colored marker to write the names of the books of the Old Testament, one name per card, and use a fourth color to write the names of the New Testament books on cards.

1 CLOTHESLINE SCRAMBLE

Stretch a clothesline across an archway, garage-door opening, or between two trees in the backyard.

2 Lay out all the cards on a table, sidewalk, or driveway.

3 Use clothespins to hang the cards on the line in order, using the divisions and the books in them. Use a stopwatch to see who finishes the fastest. Pick a different person in the family to keep time for each race so everyone gets to play.

TABLE SCRAMBLE 1

Lay the cards labeled "Old Testament" and "New Testament" on a table. Next, mix up the cards bearing the division names. Then, using a timer, see who can be first to put them in order under the Old and New Testament cards before time runs out. As you get better at it, shorten the time allowed.

Now try it with all the books of **2** the Old Testament.

Try it with all the books of **3** the New Testament.

respect for the Book

If words are symbols of ideas we want to share, then the Bible—that familiar book—is a tangible symbol of the truth of God's eternal Word. Work together as a family to keep the Bible a sacred and revered object in your home. Respect for the Book will help to teach children and remind adults that its words are God's.

💜 Keep the Bible out on a table or nightstand where it can be seen and easily picked up throughout the day.

💜 Never let dust collect on the Bible. Using it often should help keep it dustfree; if your family goes on vacation, be sure the Bible gets dusted along with the furniture when you return.

💜 Try never to pile magazines, newspapers, or other books on top of the Bible. Its words are the supreme authority in our lives, so it should be given the primary place in our homes.

💜 As soon as children begin to read, choose an important day to give them a Bible of their own. If possible, have their names printed on the cover.

💜 Choose an edition appropriate to their age and give them other copies, appropriate to each maturity level, as they mature. (See the resources section for a listing of age-appropriate editions.)

💜 Pack a Bible each time your family goes on a trip. Unpack it first when you arrive at your destination and put it where it can be seen and used.

💜 Teach little children to hold the Bible carefully and never tear or misuse it. Avoid dropping it or setting drinks or food on it.

💜 Keep a durable copy of the Bible in the car to read when you are stuck in traffic or have to wait for someone to finish an appointment.

💜 Parents should each have, treasure, and use their own favorite copies of the Bible so that children learn early that the Bible is an important guide for daily living.

💜 Read it together as a family every day. Choose a time when the family can be together such as at breakfast, suppertime, or bedtime.

keep God's day Holy THE FOURTH COMMANDMENT

The fourth commandment from God was to keep a holy day each week that was sacred—different and separate from the other days. When Jesus came He said we would not get rid of this commandment but let it affect all our other days by recognizing that all the time we are given, every day, is sacred—a gift from God's hand—and that we should treat and live each day with gratitude and respect.

Because Jesus arose from the tomb on the first day of the week, most Christians celebrate that day as the special day to keep holy and separate. Here are some ways your family can "remember the Sabbath day to keep it holy."

❤ Go together to a place of worship and join other believers in singing, worshiping, and learning about God.

❤ Try to avoid arguments, cross words, or bickering on God's special day.

❤ Eat together as a family; invite others who need to be with a family (those who are alone or away from home) to join your family.

❤ Don't work on this day. God said it was to be a day to rest our bodies, minds, and spirits.

❤ Don't shop on this day. Even though many stores are open on Sunday, get your shopping done on another day so that the Lord's day is not used for commerce.

❤ Honor God by agreeing not to play secular music on the Lord's day. Use this day to listen to Christian recordings and to sing together hymns and spiritual songs for encouragement.

❤ Enjoy God's creation and take time to really notice the sky, the grass, the birds, the trees, and all the beauty we rush by on other days. Take walks alone or with your family and take deep breaths of fresh air.

❤ Rest. Take a nap and let your body and mind restore themselves. Read a good book about God's goodness in someone's life or read poetry and stories that are uplifting.

❤ Take time for good conversation with relatives, old and young, and friends. Don't hurry. If it's good weather, "sit a spell" on the front porch, the deck, or in the garden.

❤ Focus on positive things. Think of as many things as possible for which you are genuinely thankful.

❤ Read God's Word aloud together and talk about a Bible story.

❤ Sleep well.

Our names are very important to our identities. Most of us have names that were carefully chosen by our parents. But we have other names, too, that tell something about us. For example, your name may be Benjamin, which means "much beloved and favored son." But you are also "friend," "brother," "grandson," "nephew," "third baseman," "student," and "violinist."

God's name is very important. At first, it was a word so awesome no one was allowed to pronounce it, so it had no vowels. *YHWH* was all that was written, and it meant "I am that I am." When God did allow His name to be pronounced it was *Yahweh*, or *Jehovah*. Scripture also gives God other names that have to do with His characteristics, or qualities.

revering God's name

There is actually a quality of God to meet every need we might have because God is all-sufficient. Here are some names given to God in the Scripture beside this main name—Yahweh—and the meaning or quality of each name:

- ❤ **Jehovah Jireh**
  Wonderful Counselor
  Emmanuel

- ❤ **Jehovah Rapha**
  The Mighty God
  Healer

- ❤ **El Shaddai**
  Everlasting Father
  Redeemer

1 At a stationery store buy nametags or labels that have self-stick backs.

2 Give several to each member of your family and have everyone write his or her "main name" with a black marker.

3 Then in other colors of ink, make nametags that reflect all the other names each person might go by, such as "aunt," "driver," "secretary," "Dad," "safety patrol," "tennis champ," etc.

4 Now give each person several more nametags on which to write God's main name and His other names such as "Counselor," "Jehovah Rapha," "Prince of Peace," "Comforter," etc.

5 Think together of a need you might have in your life or your family that would be met by a quality of God such as "Counselor."

6 Each of you take all your nametags to your room. When you face a particular problem, write it down on a sheet of paper or a page in your prayer journal, then put the nametag that identifies the quality of God that specifically addresses that personal need on that page.

7 Pray together, focusing on God's promise to *be* what we need, no matter what that is.

8 Remember: "God shall supply all your needs according to His riches in glory by Christ Jesus" (Phil. 4:19 NKJV).

Bible verse gift cards

1 Write a Bible verse on a recipe or greeting card that is appropriate to the holiday or the occasion.

2 Decorate it with age-appropriate artwork.

3 Tape it to a gift or mail it to the person in a separate envelope.

4 Give a photo album for the card collection as a gift.

5 Memorize the verse.

6 Discuss the verse you wrote on the card and describe how it relates to this special passage in the person's life.

gifts that honor God and others

Kids always need financial support for a special project. Parents and grandparents are often asked to buy magazines, candy, candles, or fruit, to name just a few typical fund-raisers. There is a much better way to donate to children's good causes. Donate ten dollars for every Christian biography your children or grandchildren will read and discuss with you. People like John Wesley, David Livingstone, and Corrie ten Boom will become your grandchildren's heroes, and their love for reading will also increase. You can't put a price on that! And they will be supporting your favorite cause—helping them grow as Christians.

"He that giveth, let him do it with simplicity" (Rom. 12:8 KJV).

1
For each biography read, discuss with your child or grandchild the statement or tone of that person's life. Choose together the Scripture verse that best epitomizes that life's statement. Memorize it together.

2
Use brightly colored tape to mark the spine of each book you read. On the tape use a marker to write the Scripture reference you have chosen and learned together.

3
Let the child choose special "causes" he or she feels can really make a difference and encourage him or her to donate all or a portion of the "book savings" to it.

4
Talk about other ways each of us, beginning at very early ages, can live our lives so we make a difference for the kingdom of God.

teachable moments

A "Bread of Life" Promise Box

"I am the living bread that came down from heaven. If anyone eats of this bread, he will live forever. This bread is my flesh, which I will give for the life of the world" (John 6:51 NIV).

Many of us have grown up with a little brown, plastic "Bread of Life" promise box as a permanent fixture on the kitchen table. On and off through the years we were encouraged to pull out a promise before the mealtime prayer and read it aloud. Sometimes it would get put away in a cabinet until a family crisis came up, then Mom or Dad would say, "Where is that little loaf of bread? We need a promise to stand on today!" Judy Newman of Hawthorne, New Jersey, remembers it this way:

The year began normally for us five children, Grandma, and our dear, loving, and godly parents, but this was soon to change.

Early in February my dad was diagnosed with cancer. Mom ever so lovingly cared for him and all of us. In June my eleven-year-old brother was fatally hit by a car. How thankful we were that we knew he loved and knew the Savior. Several months later my dad lost his business and had a heart attack. Needless to say, these were stormy days.

Through all of this Mom and Daddy were very concerned for our spiritual well-being. That was the year the little loaf of bread, filled with two hundred promises from the Bible, ended up on our kitchen table. The idea of having each one of us read a verse before each meal soon became as much a part of our meal as the physical food. Over the years we learned many Bible verses, and the Spirit of God has blessed each of us.

a "God's Word is..." party

1 Have a large table ready with a pretty cloth on it. Place the largest family Bible you can find in the center of the table.

2 Invite friends to come to a party bringing, as their "entrance fee," one object that the Bible says God's Word is to our lives. Make sure they bring the reference too.

Examples:

- 💜 lamp (flashlight, lantern)
- 💜 seed
- 💜 ruler or yardstick
- 💜 shield

- 💜 a song (sheet of music)
- 💜 eraser
- 💜 water
- 💜 bread
- 💜 band-aid
- 💜 dough with yeast in it
- 💜 traffic warning sign
- 💜 milk
- 💜 honey

3 As guests arrive, have them place their objects on the table.

4 After playing get-acquainted games or other recreation, have everyone gather around the table. Ask each guest to hold up the object he or she brought and ask if anyone can quote the verse from the Bible that compares this object to God's Word. The person who guesses gets to show his or her object next. If nobody guesses, the guest who brought the object reads the verse aloud. Then he or she gets to choose who goes next.

5 Serve refreshments.

stamp it on your heart

Next time you go shopping, take your list of Bible memory verses with you to a store that sells rubber stamps. These popular stamps have sprung up all over the country and are quite wonderful. You can find almost every kind of person, place, or thing on 2 x 4 block stamps.

Your family will have fun matching the Bible verses to the pictures on the stamps. The associations will be personal and thus have their own long-lasting meanings. You can make a variety of craft items with the stamps as Bible verse reminders to scatter around the house or to give as gifts.

Examples:

 "Do not let your left hand know what your right hand is doing" (Matt. 6:3 NKJV).

 "The Lamb of God, who takes away the sin of the world!" (John 1:29).

 "Love the Lord your God with all your heart" (Matt. 22:37).

 "As for me and my house, we will serve the LORD" (Josh. 24:15 NKJV).

"Consider the lilies of the field" (Matt. 6:28 NKJV).

"He who has ears to hear, let him hear!" (Matt. 11:15 NKJV).

Jesus calls real people

People learn about Jesus in many different ways. Sometimes it is through a book they read or a friend who talks about Jesus or even songs on the radio that tell of Jesus' love. There are churches in every town that try to share the Good News in their neighborhoods.

Once people learn about Jesus, they have many different responses. Some don't believe what they are told and doubt that the Bible is true. Others want to believe, but they have to think it over for a while. Here are some ideas to help you understand how Jesus calls people.

Using a Riddle
💜 Read John 3:1–8.
Often Jesus spoke in riddles. Sometimes He would say, "You people who can hear me, listen!" (Matt. 11:15). What did He mean? Can you think of times when Jesus spoke to a lot of people but only a few heard or figured out what He was saying?

Calling the First Disciples
💜 Read Matthew 4:18–22 and Mark 1:14–20.

*A disciple is a follower who learns from someone.
How did each of the disciples respond?*

Choosing the Twelve Apostles
💜 Read Luke 6:13–16.
An apostle is one who is sent to tell the Good News.
Memorize the names of the twelve apostles.

Telling a Story
💜 Read Luke 10:25–37.
Sometimes Jesus calls us to a new direction or lifestyle. Can you think of other times when Jesus told a story to call people to a new way of life?

43

"real people" interviews BECOME AN ACE REPORTER

1 Make a list of twelve people you know who are followers of Jesus (teachers, friends, relatives). From your list choose some you would like to interview and ask if they would meet with you.

2 Find a tape recorder with a good microphone.

3 Write the following interview questions on 3 x 5 cards to carry along with you.

4 Tape record your interviews and share your reports at home, school, or church.

Interview questions:

💜 What kind of person were you before you met Jesus?

💜 Where were you when you first heard about Jesus?

💜 Please share what you can recall about that time.

💜 What were your thoughts about all that Jesus promised?

💜 Did it take you very long to decide to follow Him?

💜 Tell me about your time of decision.

💜 How are you different today?

💜 What do you do, as His follower, to share the

💜 Good News?

The Empty Milk Carton

teachable moments

"But someone may ask, 'How are the dead raised? What kind of body will they have?'" (1 Cor. 15:35).

"What happens to you when you die?" The Sunday school teacher had a tough question from the second grade class. Mrs. Howell had asked for some time to consider her answer and had thought carefully about it all week. She prayed for wisdom to help teach the truths of God's Word to these tender, young, inquiring minds. God had helped her in the past, and she knew He would help her again. Sure enough, by Friday a simple object lesson began to form in her thoughts. On Sunday she went to class armed and ready.

"How many of you have ever visited a funeral home?" she asked the children. Some of them raised their hands.

"What did you see?" she continued.

"I saw my uncle in his new blue suit lying in a big silver box," volunteered Kayla. "My daddy said he went to heaven, but I don't know how he got there."

"Kayla, your uncle's *soul* went to heaven," said Mrs. Howell.

"What's a soul?" asked Jason with a puzzled look.

"A person's soul is his whole being on the inside, Jason," she explained. "It is a person's thoughts, feelings, and spirit."

Mrs. Howell took something out of her bag and put it on the table. "What is this?" she asked.

In unison they agreed, "It's a carton of milk!"

Mrs. Howell carefully opened the carton. She poured the milk into a bowl and set it aside. She sealed the carton and set it back in the same spot. "Now what is it?"

The children looked curiously at the object. Hesitantly one said, "It's a carton of milk."

"No, it's not," said another. "It's just a carton." "Yes," said another, "it's a carton . . . a carton of nothing . . . a carton of air!"

"Does it look the same?" asked the teacher.

"Yes!" they responded.

"Is it the same?" she urged.

"No, it's empty!" said Kayla. "Mrs. Howell, does that mean my uncle is empty?"

"Yes, Kayla, it means his body may look the same, but his thoughts, feelings, and spirit are alive somewhere else."

"In heaven!" Jason yelled. The class cheered with excitement. A light of understanding ever so gently dawned upon their young minds and hearts.

"Boys and girls, I want you to remember one very important thing," continued Mrs. Howell. "Someday you may get a call saying Mrs. Howell has died. You may go with your parents to see my body at the funeral home. If you do, will you remember our talk today? Will you rejoice with me that I will be only an empty carton? My soul will be with Jesus, and I will be filled with joy!"

All the children promised they would remember. And faith took a giant step forward.

Obey all his rules and commands . . .

so that you will live a long time.

Deuteronomy 6:2

*S*ome of God's rules are designed to help us live a long time on

this earth. These rules help us not to hurt each other and to not

hurt ourselves or destroy our bodies. Some of God's rules are to

protect our hearts, so our spirits don't get sick.

Some of God's rules are intended to help us live longer than this life and get to

spend eternity with Him, where no one gets sick or hurt or sad anymore. When

God says we should obey so we will live a long time . . . He also means forever.

Let's have fun hiding God's "live-long" rules in our hearts!

Section 3

for long life

LEARNING GOD'S INSTRUCTIONS

Lord, make me clean

Taking a shower or bath should be something we do every day. When we are really dirty, we know it . . . we even smell bad! Most of us take for granted that we will have hot water, fragrant soap, and fresh, clean towels in the bathroom when we need them. When was the last time you said, "Thank You, Lord, for soap and water"?

The Bible talks about the importance of being clean on the outside and on the inside. When our hearts are full of sin, we feel dirty and sad. Only the blood of Jesus can wash our hearts clean. The psalmist David said, "Wash me, and I will be whiter than snow" (Ps. 51:7 NIV). When Jesus wanted to wash Peter's feet at the Last Supper, Peter refused. Jesus answered, "Unless I wash you, you have no part with me" (John 13:8 NIV).

Shower Verse Cards

There are many Bible verses about cleansing and being clean. A good way to learn them is to make laminated verse cards for the shower or bathtub.

1 On 5 x 7 cards write some of the verses listed below.

2 Cover the cards with lamination sheets (available at most office-supply stores).

3 Punch a hole in the cards, string them together with yarn, and hang the collection in the shower or bathtub.

4 Turn up a new card each week.

5 Quiz one another at breakfast on the verse and discuss the meaning.

Bible Verses on Cleansing:

Psalm 19:12 (KJV)	Matthew 8:2 (KJV)	Titus 3:5
Psalm 51:2	Acts 10:15	Hebrews 10:22
Psalm 119:9 (KJV)	Acts 22:16	James 4:8
Isaiah 1:16,25	1 Corinthians 6:11	1 John 1:7,9 (KJV)
Jeremiah 4:14	Ephesians 5:25–27	

Bath Song

Words and Music by
Robert C. Evans

When I take a bath, (When I take a bath) I think a-bout the Lord. (I think a-bout the Lord) And how He washed a-way my sin. (And how He washed a-way my sin) Let me tell you more. (Let me tell you more) 1. He washed my hands so I could touch, (He washed my hands so I could touch) the world he loved so ver-y much. (The world he loved so ver-y much) Je-sus fills me up with hope, (Je-sus fills me up with hope) and wash-es me with su-per soap! (And wash-es me with su-per soap!)

Verse 2:
He washed my feet so I could walk
And give a happy gospel talk.

Verse 3:
He washed my face so I could smile
And tell the world I am His child.

1 rub imaginary bar of soap
2 "wash" as appropriate
3 start hands at knees, bring up body, lift over head
4 bring hands quickly down to knees, scrubbing as you go

The Rewards of Baby-sitting

Every day after school Josh had to hurry home to watch his six-year-old sister, Pam. It was no fun! All the other guys got to hang out together thinking up cool things to do, but not Josh. Sometimes he thought he just couldn't take it one more day.

Josh often complained to Mrs. Wilson, an elderly neighbor. She prayed for Josh and wanted to find a way to help him. Mrs. Wilson began to call Josh every afternoon just to find out how his day had gone. He seemed to enjoy it, so she took a step of courage and asked if she could read a Bible verse to him. One day she read Colossians 3:23–24, "Whatever you do, work at it with all your heart, as working for the Lord, not for men, since you know that you will receive an inheritance from the Lord as a reward" (NIV).

They discussed this verse together. Josh realized that it was a lot easier to do his baby-sitting chores if he thought about doing it for the Lord and not just for his parents or sister. Josh discovered that serving his sister made him feel important to God. Mrs. Wilson helped him look for some of the other rewards God was giving him daily as he was faithful at home.

Do you know of a child who is home alone after school? Pray for his or her safety. Do you know of a substitute grandmother or grandfather who could phone this child regularly? Maybe you could help them know each other.

the "promise" commandment

There is only one commandment that comes with a "promise." It is the fifth commandment:

"Honor your father and your mother so that you will live a long time in the land that the LORD your God is going to give you."

(Exod. 20:12)

Why do you think God promised if we obey our parents we will have a long life?

1 Make a list of some things you can learn from your parents that could save your life, keep you safe, or increase the time and quality of your life. (Parents, you, too, have parents, so do this as a family.)

2 Now make a list of all the things God wants parents to teach their children and how each would give them a long, happy life "in the land" and even into eternity. Include suggestions for how these things could be taught.

3 Read Isaiah 54:13 and Proverbs 22:6. See Chapter 14 for other promises of God that will enrich your life if you parent well and are willing to be parented.

the transformed life

"We . . . are being transformed into His likeness" (2 Cor. 3:18 NIV).

When you give your life to Jesus, your life changes . . . your heart changes, your actions change. You are a new person!

Do you like popcorn?

Popcorn can be used as an object lesson to talk about the transformation Christ brings in one's life.

unpopped kernels—Before people become Christians their lives are hard and unusable (Heb. 3:8).

multicolored kernels—Jesus died for all people regardless of color (Acts 10:34).

oil—Represents the Holy Spirit, who brings us to repentance (Heb. 1:9).

pan—Represents the church which helps us to become all God wants us to be (Eph. 3:20–21).

heat—Represents the fires of conviction (Heb. 12:29).

popped corn—Represents a life turned completely around. Now, wearing white like a wedding dress, it symbolizes our readiness to be the bride of Christ (Rev. 19:7).

salt—We are the salt of the earth (Matt. 5:13).

no pepper—There are things that can defile and make dirty (Dan. 1:8).

kernels that won't pop—Kernels that do not pop are like those who refuse to come to Christ (John 3:36).

Why not make some delicious, white, fluffy popcorn for a snack right now! Share it with a friend. Share, too, how the Lord is using you since He changed your heart and life.

If you were on a boat and a man fell overboard, what could you do? You could jump in the water and try to save him, or you could throw him a lifesaver, or life preserver. A life preserver is a buoyant device, usually in the shape of a ring, designed to keep a person afloat in the water. It is tied to a "lifeline" that is securely fastened to the boat, so the person can be pulled to safety.

Using Candy Lifesavers to Teach the Lesson

can a lifesaver save your life?

We can use the colors of candy Lifesavers to remind us of Jesus, our "Life Saver."

RED stands for the blood of Jesus, shed for you and me. "His blood cleanses us from all sin" (1 John 1:7).

WHITE is for the cleansing of our sin on Calvary. "Wash me, and I shall be whiter than snow" (Ps. 51:7 NKJV).

GREEN is for the Christian growth that draws us closer to Jesus and the eternal life we're promised (see Eph. 3:16–21).

YELLOW is for the streets of gold we can't wait to see (see Rev. 21:21).

ORANGE is for "orange" you glad you've got a real LIFE SAVER!

We can tell others about our "Life Saver," but they must choose to take hold of Him for themselves. Jesus offers the Life Line to each one of us. He wants to keep us afloat on the sea of life.

Today would be a good day to share your Life Saver with a friend. Someone you know may be yelling "HELP!" Can you hear someone calling?

the "scripture-memory off" challenge

The kind of competition the Bible encourages is to outdo each other in serving and loving each other. Make a family contest of learning God's Word so your love and service will have a strong biblical base. When we compete in hiding God's Word in our hearts, there are never any losers.

1 Choose a week (it can be a holiday time such as Christmas or Lent, or a regular week of each month) to review and memorize as many Bible verses as possible.

2 Collect prizes that you know will be a hit with your family members.

3 During the competition the first person quotes a verse. Each person must then quote a different verse.

4 When it is your turn, if you can't quote a verse that has not already been quoted, you are out of the round.

5 Keep score of how many verses each person recites and award a daily winner. Give a double score to younger players.

6 Add up each person's score for the week and award a grand prize winner.

Encourage players to find Scripture verses to memorize that their siblings or parents might not know, so when it's time for the finals, each will have a better chance of winning.

teachable moments

Bible Verse Time for Two-Year-Olds

It's never too early to begin hiding the Word in children's hearts. "Our two-year-old, Ellen, has an excellent memory, and we have 'Bible verse time' every day," says Cheri Steinbrinck of Green Bay, Wisconsin.

Here is the plan Cheri uses with Ellen:

- Say the whole verse with the reference at the beginning and at the end.
- Say a few words at a time and let the child repeat them phrase by phrase until you finish the verse.
- Play "fill in the blank" with one word, then two, and so on until the child learns it all.
- By the end of the week have the child say it alone.
- Review the Bible verse often.

Do two-year-olds understand the Bible verses they learn?

Paula Podgurski's son is two and a half years old. He can recite Psalm 23, Psalm 100, and the Lord's Prayer all by himself. Paula writes from Haledon, New Jersey: "Of course, he doesn't understand the meaning of all of the words he is reciting, but he will eventually. In the meantime he's opening his spirit to God's dealings and power in his life. He often interrupts me to ask the meaning of a word, so his vocabulary is improving at the same time."

alphabetical Bible collection

1 Buy everyone in the family an inexpensive address book.

2 Record the Bible verses you want to learn alphabetically.

For example:

D—*Delight* and *desire*—"Delight yourself in the Lord and He will give you the desires of your heart" (Ps. 37:4 NKJV).

F—*Follow*—"Follow me, and I will make you fishers of men" (Matt. 4:19 KJV).

3 Carry your Bible alphabet "book" with you when you have to be away (for camp, visits, college, military service, business trips) to give you quick encouragement and wisdom in new situations. Having God's Word as a quiet reference will enrich your days and lift your spirits if you run into problems.

4 Take these Bible alphabet books on family trips so you can record verses as you play the Alphabet Race Game. The first person recites an "A" verse; the next person says a "B" verse, and so on until you've gone through the alphabet. Give a promise prize to the first one to write a verse corresponding to each letter of the alphabet.

Bible medicine for a healthy spirit
(AND BODY, TOO)

Doctors are now sure that our attitudes directly affect our physical health. Here is a list of attitudes that are directly related to common illness.

Attitudes	Diseases
anger	ulcers
frustration	stress on the heart
worry	circulatory disease
stress	headaches
guilt	eating disorders
holding grudges	sleeplessness
prolonged sadness	muscle tension
too much self-pity	digestive disorders

God's Word has a lot to say about keeping our spirits and attitudes healthy. Here is a way to "internalize" God's "vitamins" for healthy attitudes and bodies.

1 Type or write God's healthy instructive verses (see list) on strips of paper, roll them up tightly, and seal each one with a drop of rubber cement. Hold the "scroll" intact with a twist tie until the cement dries.

2 Place the scrolls in a small box like the ones jewelry comes in or in a velvet "watch box."

3 Keep the box on your night-stand.

4 Each night before going to sleep, "take" one vitamin verse. Open the scroll; read God's instructions several times, and think about it. Try to put it in your memory bank.

♥ Go to sleep thinking about the verse instead of all the negative things that might have made you angry, frustrated, or stressed that day.

♥ Here are some examples of spiritual medicine from the New King James Version of the Bible:

♥ "I can do all things through Christ who strengthens me" (Phil 4:1).

♥ "Jesus said . . .'I am the way, the truth, and the life. No one comes to the Father except through me'" (John 14:6).

♥ "I will never leave you nor forsake you" (Heb. 13:5b).

♥ "If we confess our sins, He is faithful and just to forgive us our sins and to cleanse us from all unrighteousness"(1 John 1:9).

♥ "God is faithful, by whom you were called into the fellowship of His Son, Jesus Christ our Lord" (1 Cor. 1:9).

♥ "This is the message which we have heard from Him and declare to you, that God is light and in Him there is no darkness at all" (1 John 1:15).

♥ "The LORD is merciful and gracious" (Ps. 103:8).

♥ "The Lord is . . . slow to anger and great in mercy" (Ps. 145:8).

♥ "And my God shall supply all your need according to His riches in glory by Christ Jesus" (Phil. 4:19).

maturity test

Did anyone in your family ever say, "Oh, grow up!" or did you ever complain, "You treat me like a child!" Maturity is often, but not always, a result of getting older. Some people who are old enough to be mature are *very* immature. Here is a list of things by which you can measure your maturity. You might like to write this list on a big sheet of construction paper and put it on the refrigerator or on the back door so you can keep testing your maturity every day. (By the way, my mother made up this list for our family!—*Gloria*)

- If someone trusts you—earn it.
- If someone speaks to you—answer.
- If you want to be respected—be respectful.
- If you make a mistake—admit it.
- If you are hired to work—don't shirk.
- If you make a promise—keep it. (Don't readily make promises you may not be able to keep.)
- If you borrow it—return it.
- If you open it—close it. (Leave things as you find them unless otherwise instructed.)
- If you break it—fix it.
- If you lose it—find it or replace it.
- Keep clean—if you do not respect yourself no one else will.

The home, the church, the school, business, commerce, communications, and politics are all in great need of people who are mature. If you are dependable, someone will find you.

Here are some "maturity" verses for your family to memorize or study:

Deuteronomy 7:21–24	Philippians 1:6
Matthew 14:23–24	Titus 2:11–15
Mark 4:26–29	Hebrews 5:12 and 6:1–2
John 4:13–15	1 John 2:12–13
2 Corinthians 13:8–9	

"love the Lord with all your heart"

(Jesus' words in Matthew 22:37)

Think about your heart. There is your physical heart, which is a muscle inside your chest. It pumps blood to all the parts of your body. Then there is your emotional heart through which you experience feelings. Sometimes you have a happy heart, and other times your heart feels sad.

The word *heart* in the Bible usually means the place of feelings or the center of your very personhood. Look at these verses about the heart: Deuteronomy 30:10–17; Psalm 26:2; Proverbs 15:13–15; Mark 12:30; Luke 2:19 (NIV), 6:45, and 24:25 (KJV); Acts 2:46.

What does it mean to "invite Jesus into your heart"?

What does it mean to invite someone into your house? Usually you think about the people you want to invite and why you would like them to visit. Sometimes you send them a written invitation. When they come, you plan your time so you can visit with them and enjoy their company. Often you share your feelings with them. Friends help friends in need. Good friendships last throughout the years and make your life better.

Invite Jesus to be your friend

1 Think about why you want Jesus to be your friend.

2 Write out an invitation to Jesus to be with you.

3 Plan the time you will give during your day to spend with Jesus.

4 What feelings or needs do you want to share with Him?

Jesus wants to be your best friend for life. The way to let Him do that is to invite Him into your heart, the center of your being. He can turn sad hearts into happy hearts.

Special Gifts from Grandma
The Gift of God's Word

Most of us have had the experience of spending hours looking for just the right gift for a very special person. Have you ever noticed that grandparents can be the best gift givers? Maybe they have more time to shop, or maybe they have more experience in the real values of life.

"My mother gives all her grandchildren a verse from the Bible on special occasions (birthdays, Easter, Valentine's Day, etc.)," shares Jayne Conley of Wrenshall, Minnesota. "The children save them and look at them often. It encourages them to learn the verse because they know it was picked out especially for them by their grandmother."

Obey all his rules and commands so . . .
All will go well for you,
and you will become a great nation
in a fertile land, just as the LORD,
the God of your ancestors,
has promised you.

Deuteronomy 6:2–3

*G*od wants His children to get along with each other so

we can avoid conflict, ugliness, and pain. His Word tells us

ways we can bless and encourage each other. It shows us

ways to bring out the best in each other and help develop the

special abilities God has given to each person.

God also intends for His children to live in harmony with

creation and the land. If we do, the land will feed us, protect

us, shelter us, and give us much pleasure. But in

turn we must protect, nurture, and respect the land.

Here are some wonderful ways God has provided for us to get along with

each other and our environment. By heeding God's instructions we will be able to

pass on to our children—and our children's children—our rewarding

relationship with the good earth and those who share it with us.

Section 4

LEARNING WAYS TO GET ALONG WITH . . . .

others and our environment

Ephesians 4, 5, and 6 and Romans 12 are "behavior chapters" describing how each of us wants and needs to be treated and how we should treat each other. More important than our roles as earthly family members, we are all—parents and kids alike—*siblings in the family of God.* We may feel that there is a big

giving what we need

difference between parents and kids, between children and adults. But in reality, all of us have the same needs, and we are here to meet each other's needs. Ephesians 5:21 says we honor Christ by submitting to (or meeting the needs of) each other.

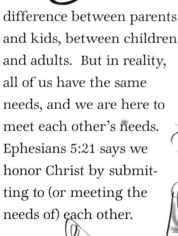

1 Study together Ephesians 4, 5, and 6 and Romans 12 in the New Century, New King James, Living Bible, or New International versions, thinking of the words as applying to family—specifically, *your* family.

2 Compare the two lists and talk about each other's needs and how they could be met in your family.

3 Tell each other how you feel when one of these needs is ignored. For example, how do parents feel when kids always expect to be loved and appreciated but never remember to say thank you for special thoughtfulness, favors, or kindness from their

parents (no. 9 on the parents' list)? How do kids feel when parents are always changing their minds (or do not agree) on where the limits are, what is permitted, and what is a "no-no" (no. 6 on the kids' list)?

4 Compare the lists again and see how similar they are. This is because we are all human, siblings in God's family, and we need the same things. We also need to be able to *give* what we *need.*

5 See if you can find verses in the Bible that apply to each item on both lists.

6 Pray together for more sensitivity to each other's needs and for helpful ways to meet those needs.

What Do Children Need?

1. Acceptance
2. Praise and appreciation
3. To learn they can trust their parents not to deceive them or break promises
4. Consistency and fairness
5. To feel that their fears, their desires, their feelings, their inexplicable impulses, their frustrations, and their inabilties are understood by their parents
6. To know exactly where the limits are—what is permitted and what is prohibited
7. To know that home is a safe place, a place of refuge
8. Warm approval when they do well
9. Firm correction when they do wrong
10. To know that their parents are stronger than they are, able to weather the storms and dangers of the outer world, and able to stand up to their children's rages and unreasonable demands
11. To feel their parents like them and *want to* and *will* take time to listen
12. Perceptive responses to their growing needs for independence
13. To be hugged and noticed

What Do Parents Need?

1. Acceptance
2. Praise and appreciation
3. To know that their trust in their children is not being betrayed
4. To know they are being told the truth and receiving honest communication
5. To know their children are learning to gradually be givers, not just takers, that they're not being used, played against each other, or manipulated
6. To feel that when they try to be fair and just their trust will not be greeted with defiance and rebellion
7. To feel that the whole family is working at making the home a place of safety and refuge
8. To have their children grow mature enough to disagree in a loving way, without becoming belligerent and disrespectful
9. To have their giving and love appreciated, not taken for granted
10. To realize that protecting their marriage and romance is to everyone's advantage
11. To be hugged and noticed

"dominion" also means "responsibility"

As a part of God's great love for us, He trusted us (because He made us only a little lower than the angels) with caring for the wonder of His awesome creation. Study carefully Psalm 8. Read it in several translations.

Caring for creation is a reward from God for being His most trusted friends. It may also be intended to keep us intimate with the amazing workings and habits of nature, so we will never be able to forget that the majesty and glory of Jehovah, our Lord, fills the whole earth.

God gave us instructions for being good caretakers of His creation:

♥ Take care of animals.
"A good man is concerned for the welfare of his animals" (Prov. 12:10 TLB).

♥ Give the soil a rest.
"Sow and reap your crops for six years, but let the land rest and lie fallow during the seventh year, and let the poor among the people harvest any volunteer crop that may come up" (Exod. 23:10–11 TLB).

♥ Let the animals find food.
"Leave the rest [grain of the harvest] for the animals to enjoy. The same rule applies to your vineyards [grapes] and your olive groves" (Exod. 23:11 TLB).

❤ Don't overwork your animals; give them a rest.

"Work six days only, and rest the seventh; this is to give your oxen and donkeys a rest, as well as the people of your household—your slaves (employees) and visitors" (Exod. 23:12 TLB).

❤ Take care of lost animals.

"If you see your fellow Israelite's ox or sheep wandering away, don't ignore it. Take it back to its owner. If the owner does not live close to you, or if you do not know who the owner is, take the animal home with you. Keep it until the owner comes looking for it; then give it back" (Deut. 22:1–2).

❤ Help injured animals.

"If you see your fellow Israelite's donkey or ox fallen on the road, don't ignore it. Help the owner get it up" (Deut. 22:4).

❤ Don't misuse animals.

"Don't plow with an ox and a donkey tied together . . . . When an ox is working in the grain, do not cover its mouth to keep it from eating" (Deut. 22:10 and 25:4).

Respect all creatures and the habitats God planned for them, for these are God's property.
"The earth belongs to the LORD, and everything in it" (Psalm 24:1).

Talk together about ways your family can care for your pets and other animals around your property as if God Himself had left you in charge of them for Him. He has!

nature awareness

Even very young children, including babies, can begin to experience nature and develop a love for God's creation. Here are some ways to keep the whole family tuned in to God's voice and the wonders He has made.

Feel the wind. Run across a hillside or along a path in the park, then talk about the wind. Be thankful for the marvel of skin and nerve endings that let you feel the breeze. Make kites and see the wind takes them high into the heavens. Swing together on a swing set and focus on the joy of invisible wind. With older children study the principles of aerodynamics that can lift a 747 into the air. Put up windsocks to observe how wind currents change direction.

Read together these verses about the wind and its qualities:

Psalm 1:4	Amos 4:13
Psalm 147:18	John 3:8
Proverbs 11:29	Acts 2:2
Song of Solomon 4:16	Ephesians 4:4
Isaiah 41:13-16	

Enjoy the day and the night. Watch the sun come up and go down and see God's amazing "light show." Feel its warmth on your skin. Why do you feel "down" when you can't see the sun? Is the sun shining just as brightly, even when clouds get in the way? What happens to plants when we put them in the sun? In the dark? But what would happen if there was hot sun all the time? Talk about and observe God's balance in nature.

Read together:

Genesis 1:5	Psalm 136:8
Psalm 19	Isa 60:19
Psalm 42:8	Matthew 5:45
Psalm 77:6	Ephesians 4:26
Psalm 104:20	Revelation 21:25
Psalm 121:6	Revelation 22:5

Observe and appreciate the stars, moon, and constellations. Sit or lie on a blanket outside on a porch or a second-story deck and try to count the stars. Watch the moon at different times of the month to see how it changes. Talk about the moon's effect on the tides, the seasons, and gravity. If a special celestial event (a comet, a lunar eclipse, a very bright planet, a meteor shower) is about to occur, set your alarm clock and get everyone out of bed. Fix a snack (like crackers and milk) and watch it. (Take blankets out to keep everyone warm.) Talk about the great lights God created to rule the night and the day.

Read together:

Numbers 24:17	Psalm 136:9
Psalm 8:3	Psalm 148:3
Psalm 72:7	Matthew 2:2
Psalm 89:37	Hebrews 11:12
Psalm 104:19	Revelation 8:10–11

Animal homing habits. Find an empty nest and observe how it is made. Watch a pair of swans building a nest and note how the cob (the father) is involved in its construction.

Observe squirrel "houses" in bare winter trees. Notice hornets' amazing nests. Find foxholes and rabbits' burrows. If you live in or visit a prairie, observe prairie dogs' "communities." Watch beavers and muskrats building dams and burrowing into creekbanks. Find an eagle or stork's nest with binoculars. Watch a bee colony or an ant community building their hives and hills. Make a scrapbook (with photographs) of as many animal dwellings as you can find, including some "people dwellings."

Read together:

Matthew 8:20	Isaiah 7:14–25
Psalm 84:3	Psalm 104:21–22
Luke 9:58	Proverbs 6:6
Jeremiah 22:23	Jeremiah 29:16
Job 37:8	Job 39:27
Psalm 104:10–11	Psalm 104:17
Psalm 148:10	Psalm 104:18

Observe and learn the names of flowers, trees, and grasses.
Make a collection of leaves, pressed wildflowers, seeds, nuts, pods, or bark. As you drive on the highway, through state parks, or in the country, make a list together of the different kinds of trees you see; list them by name. Take closeup photographs of rare or endangered wildflowers and glue them to 5 x 7 cards with a note about where each flower was growing and under what conditions, including the time of year.

Read together:

Genesis 1:11	Genesis 8:22
Psalm 126:6	Matthew 13:38
Matthew 7:17-18	Matthew 12:33
Psalm 103:15	Song of Solomon 2:12
Luke 8:11	Psalm 148:9
1 Corinthians 9:10	Revelation 22:2, 14
Psalm 1:3	Luke 21:29
Isaiah 55:12	

It is not easy to create something out of nothing. To help your family appreciate God our Creator, give everyone an "ingenuity bag" and try to design your own creation. The only instruction is that whatever each person creates should depict something found in the Bible.

"In the beginning God created the heaven and the earth" (Gen. 1:1 KJV).

the ingenuity bag

Ingenuity Bag

1

Put the following items in a brown paper lunch sack:

- ♥ 1 paper plate
- ♥ 1 piece of fabric
- ♥ 1 paper clip
- ♥ 1 piece of chewing gum
- ♥ 1 drinking straw
- ♥ 1 safety pin
- ♥ 1 file card
- ♥ 1 rubber band
- ♥ 3 notebook hole rein forcements
- ♥ 2 toothpicks

2

Each person may use glue, staples, crayons, and markers as needed. No other items can be added. Use one or all of the items in the bag including the bag itself.

3

Set a time limit for this activity. When time is out, discuss the following questions:

1. What does the word *ingenuity* mean? (Look it up in a dictionary.)
2. What does your creation depict?
3. What was the hardest part of being a creator?
4. How does God feel when we destroy what He has created?

Some people's trash can be another person's treasure. Most of us have a lot of things around the house that we don't use: clothes, dishes, toys, books, etc. Instead of just throwing them away, you can recycle them at a Trash-to-Treasure Redemption Party. You can do this at church with your Sunday school class or at your house with your neighbors. Here's how:

"trash-to-treasure" redemption party

Set a day at least four weeks ahead of time.

Week 1 Make invitations out of recycled items such as used napkins, lunch sacks, or can labels. Decide on a cause to which you would like to contribute the proceeds of your sale. Include this information on your invitation.

Week 2 Mail the invitations. Make banners for the front of the house or church using Matthew 10:8 as your theme: "Freely you have received, freely give" (NKJV).

Week 3

Plan several crazy door prizes for the one who:
- brings the most stuff
- gives away the most stuff
- makes the best trade of the day
- brings the most interesting leftovers

Week 4 Use trash bags to spread on the grass or to cover tables. At the party, display all of the recycled treasures. Invite guests to look over the table and choose items they would like to "rescue." They may decide what it's worth and contribute that amount to the cause. Encourage generosity by posting a sign by the collection basket.

It is more fun to give than to receive (See Acts 20:35 NKJV).

YOU ARE INVITED TO A CLEAN OUT YOUR CLOSETS, DESKS, CABINETS & GARAGES & BRING ALL ITEMS YOU DON'T USE ANYMORE FOR TRADE OR SALE AT OUR TRASH TO TREASURE PARTY

DATE:
TIME:
LOCATION:
PROCEEDS GO TO:
DRESS: WEAR CLOTHES YOU WANT TO TRASH OR TRADE

We were once worn out by sin and trashed by Satan until we were bought back at a very high price by God's Son, Jesus Christ, who gave His very life for us. The word for that is redemption. Find as many verses as you can about redemption (in a Bible concordance look up redemption, redeemed, and redeemer) and post them around the yard or on the tables.

Kids who are taught to see, appreciate, and love nature are less likely to be bored and much more likely to care for creation and to take seriously their responsibility for "having dominion." What will excite one child may not, at first, excite another, so try these ideas as a family:

the Lord's earth

♥ Collect soil samples and label the samples with the places and terrains they came from. For example: "sand—Puerto Rico beach." Call for information about the "Last Great Places" Conservatory and other natural preserves. Contact the Nature Conservancy, 1815 N. Lynn Street, Arlington, Virginia 22209 (Phone: 1 800-628-6860).

♥ Take nature walks on trails, mountains, woods, deserts, beaches, preserves and parks, and inland lake shores.

♥ Go fossil hunting.

♥ Search for animal tracks, then photograph and identify them or make plaster of Paris castings.

♥ Go bird-watching and listening. Photograph and record birds and identify them. Collect fallen feathers and abandoned nests to identify.

♥ Start collections of rocks, formations, "gems," leaves (identify and mount samples), insects, wildflowers (press, identify, and mount different species), bark (learn to identify kinds of trees by their bark), moss, algae, and lichens. Make sure you collect specimens only in areas where it is allowed.

♥ Make a study of all kinds of eggs from frogs, birds, and insects.

♥ Study and identify different species of butterflies and observe their cocoons.

♥ Study pond life and keep a journal of all the living things you can observe there. Look at pond water under a microscope and identify simple cell life.

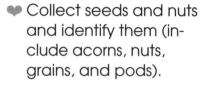

♥ Collect seeds and nuts and identify them (include acorns, nuts, grains, and pods).

♥ Collect samples of crops from a geographical area such as corn, wheat, barley, etc. (Clear baby food jars make great storage for collecting and labeling.)

♥ Go snorkeling and identify fish and sea plants.

♥ Study fish and their habits and learn to identify species when you are fishing or visiting aquariums.

Have your seen any "chlorofluorocarbons" around lately? (Some people call them CFCs for short.) You're not sure? Well, have you been to a fast-food restaurant where your food came in a polystyrene box? Or has your mom picked up some meat in the grocery store in a polystyrene packing tray? If so, you have seen some chlorofluorocarbons!

These trays and boxes are made with CFCs, chemicals that scientists believe are destroying the ozone layer in the earth's atmosphere. The ozone layer protects the earth from most of the sun's ultraviolet rays, making life on earth possible. It is a part of God's delicate balance in creation. Here are some things your family can do to help protect our environment:

o-u-t with c-f-cs!

O-U-T WITH C-F-CS!

1. Don't buy things in polysty-rene packages.

2. If you eat fast food, go to restaurants that have switched to serving food in paper wrappers or boxes, prefer-ably recycled paper to help save trees.

3. Don't buy things packaged in polystyrene "eggs" or blocks.

4. Ask the butcher in your super-market to wrap your meat or chicken in paper, not plastic.

5. Don't buy furniture with foam padding.

You can find other ideas in *How to Make the World a Better Place* by Jeffrey Hollender (William Morrow, 1990), *Caring for Creation in Your Own Backyard* by Loren and Mary Ruth Wilkinson (Servant, 1992), and *How to Rescue the Earth* by Tony Campolo (Thomas Nelson, 1992).

God put amazing variety in the land He has given us. If we learn about the land and work with it, it will be good to us and we will have a long life in it enjoying its gifts.

appreciating the land God has given us

Create a model of various kinds of land areas and learn about the special needs and products of each kind of land.

Plant a prairie:

The prairie is made up of different kinds of grasses that hold the rich soil in place and produce grains that feed people and animals. They keep the wildlife sheltered and so much more. You can learn to appreciate the prairie by planting a prairie corner in your yard. To get authentic seeds, send for the book: *Sources of Native Seeds and Plants* from the Soil and Water Conservation Society, 7517 N.E. Ankeny Road, Ankeny, Iowa 50021. The book costs three dollars and provides sources for seeds in every state. Look up "grass" or "grasses" in your concordance.

Design a desert:

The desert looks dry and still, but in reality it is active, delicately balanced, and incredibly diverse. Use an old aquarium to create a desert. Layer sand and plant desert plants in your terrarium. Most nurseries or garden-supply stores carry books and plants to help you. Find all the Bible references you can about the desert.

Cultivate a crop-bearing plot:

Choose a crop you would like to watch grow, one that will grow in your climate. Examples might be corn, wheat, rye, vegetables, soybeans, or oats. Ask your local farm bureau for seed samples and advice on planting. Use compost or bagged fertilizer to support your soil. Find Bible verses that mention planting and harvest, seeds, and grains.

A Soft Word

". . . and a little child will lead them" (Isa. 11:6).

I am a baby Christian. Having patience is new to me, but I want my children to see godly traits in me. This helps me to obey the Lord, because I can't teach them very well if I'm not living the lessons. I know they are watching me. One day my son saw I was having a bad day. He said softly, "Mom, I don't think you are building your house on the rock right now; can I pray with you?"

It is moments like this that make me know I am blessed. My son is understanding the Bible verses and songs I am teaching him. And some days he is the teacher . . . and I am the student!

—Melanie Freeman, Saint Mary's, Georgia

"don't eat these birds"

Two places in the Old Testament list the birds God told the Israelites not to eat: Deuteronomy 14:11–18 and Leviticus 11:13–19. Some of the Hebrew names of these birds would be unfamiliar to us, but Bible bird scholars have given us some ideas of what these birds are:

Hebrew text	Scholars' suggestions of present name
nester	griffon vulture, sometimes called the golden eagle
peres	bearded vulture or ossifrage
ozniyyah	short-tailed eagle or osprey
daah	black kite
ayyah	saker falcon or common vulture
oreb	raven or rook
bath yaanah	eagle owl or ostrich
tachmas	short-eared owl or nighthawk
shachaph	long-eared owl, sea gull, or cuckoo
nets	kestrel or sparrow hawk
kos	tawny owl or little owl
shalak	fisher owl or cormorant
yanshuph	screech owl, ibis, or great owl
tishemeth	little owl, water hen, or swan
qaath	scops owl or pelican
racham	osprey or vulture or gier-eagle
chasidah	stork or heron
anaphah	cormorant or heron
dukiphath	hoopoe or lapwing
atalleph	bat

See *All the Birds of the Bible* by Alice Parmalee (Keats Publishing).

The Bible often mentions the "singing," or the "call," of the birds. It also speaks of the sad sounds of the birds. You, too, can learn to recognize the language of different birds.

listening for the birds

Try to record on a tape recorder as many different bird sounds as you can and identify the "singer." You can obtain taped recordings of bird songs from nature stores or nature catalogs. Many large bookstores also carry birdsong recordings. Compare these to the birdsongs you hear in your yard or on family trips. Here are some references where bird sounds are mentioned in the Bible:

Song of Solomon 2:11-12
Ecclesiastes 12:4
Psalm 104
Micah 1:8
Isaiah 38:14
Zephaniah 2:14
Isaiah 59:11
Job 41:5
Matthew 26:34 & 74-75
Mark 13:35
Mark 14:30, 72
Luke 22:34 & 60-61
John 13:38
John 18:27
Revelation 8:13

Wonderful winged creatures fly through the pages of Scripture. Many have symbolic significance to our lives. Others simply show God's love for the birds and let us know that we can learn important lessons from them and their habits. Here are some ways your family can get acquainted with the Bible through the birds.

Start a bird sanctuary in your own backyard. Using your knowledge of feeding preferences, nest-building habits, and shelter needs of various birds, place bird feeders, nesting materials, suet holders, perching poles, and birdbaths around your yard. Plant trees, shrubs, and flowers such as sunflowers, Washington hawthorn (cardinals and cedar waxings love the red berries), Russian olive, various pines, and several small patches of seed grasses such as wheat, oats, barley, etc.

Borrow resource books on birds and their habits from the library to find out as much as possible about each bird of the Bible.

Spend several weeks of family worship time studying the birds of the Bible and the stories involving birds. Learn key verses about various birds.

family Bible bird-watching the fifth day of creation

Draw pictures on construction or drawing paper of each bird as you study it, and write at the bottom of each picture what you've learned about that bird. At the top of the picture neatly print the Bible verses referring to this bird.

Combine the pictures into a book by taping pages together punching holes and collecting them in a binder, or by pasting pictures in a bound scrapbook.

Plan a family vacation during which you will visit several bird sanctuaries, aviaries, or zoos that have ornithological collections. After each day's excursion spend time as a family discussing what you learned about the Bible birds and the wonder of God's amazing attention to the details of survival, protection, communication, and beauty in the aviary world. What does all this say to us as His human creation?

Keep notes about new things you learn from observing birds that visit your yard. Why does the Bible use each particular bird as it does in the story or reference?

Make a photo journal of your bird photos and make notes about where the pictures were taken, the times of year, location, time of day, and weather conditions.

Take walks with your family in the woods or in nearby parks or bird sanctuaries and try to spot the birds you have found in the Bible. Take binoculars and a camera. Learn about the birds' habitat, and feeding habits so you'll known where they will most likely be observed.

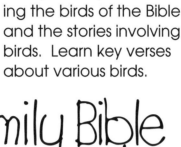

Bible references to birds

Here is a list of Bible references to birds. Are you surprised there are so many? God must consider birds a very important part of His creation. What can we learn from God's winged creatures?

Old Testament

Genesis:
1:2, 20–22
1:26, 28, 30
2:19–20
6:7, 20
7:3, 8, 14
7:21, 23
8:7, 9–12, 17
8:19–20
9:2, 10
15:9, 11
40:17, 19

Exodus:
16:13
19:4

Leviticus:
1:14–17
5:7, 11
7:26
11:13–19
11:46
12:6, 8
14:4–7
14:22, 30
14:49–53
15:14, 29
17:13
20:25

Numbers:
6:10
11:31, 32
24:21

Deuteronomy:
4:17
14:11–18, 20
22:6–7
28:26, 49
32:11

1 Samuel:
17:44, 46
26:20

2 Samuel:
1:23
21:10

1 Kings:
4:23, 33
14:11
16:4
17:4, 6

Nehemiah:
5:18

Job:
9:26
12:7
28:7, 21
30:29
35:11
38:41
39:13–18
39:26, 30
41:5

Psalms:
8:8
11:1
50:11
55:6
74:19
78:27
79:2
84:3
102:6–7
103:5
104:17
147:9
148:10

Proverbs:
1:17
6:5
7:23
23:5
26:2
27:8
30:17
30:19
30:31

Song of Solomon:
1:15
2:12, 14
4:1
5:2
5:11–12
6:9

Isaiah:
8:8
10:14
13:21
14:23
16:2
31:5
34:11, 13, 15
38:14
40:31
43:20
46:11
59:11
60:8

Jeremiah:
4:13, 25
5:26–27
7:33
8:7
9:10
12:4, 9
15:3
16:4
17:11
19:7
34:20
48:28, 40
49:16, 22
50:39

Lamentations:
3:52
4:3, 19

Ezekiel:
1:5–11
7:16
10:14
11:22
13:20
17:3, 7, 23
29:5
31:6, 13
32:4
38:20
39:4, 17
44:31

Daniel:
2:38
4:12

Hosea:
2:18
4:3
7:11–12
8:1
9:11
11:11

Amos:
3:5

Obadiah:
4

Micah:
1:16

Nahum:
2:7

Habakuk :
1:8

Zephaniah:
1:3
2:14

Zechariah:
5:9

New Testament

Matthew:
3:16
6:26
8:20
10:16, 29, 31
13:4, 32
21:12
23:37
24:28
26:34, 74–75

Mark:
14:30, 68, 72

Luke:
3:22
8:5
9:58
12:6–7
13:19, 34

John:
1:32
2:14, 16
13:38
18:27

Acts:
10:12
11:6

Romans:
1:23

1 Corinthians:
15:39

James:
3:7

Revelation:
4:7
8:13
12:14
18:2
19:17, 21

teachable moments

When Life Isn't Perfect

Our family has not been immune to the stresses and problems of today or to attacks of the enemy because of our efforts to be diligent in teaching the Word to our children. We have been horrible failures at times and completely brokenhearted at our own sins.

We have tried to show our children that it is possible to start over and go on, but only through the wonderful mercy and forgiveness of Jesus. We have told them that "God has no grandchildren." We are each responsible to "work out our own salvation with fear and trembling" (Phil. 2:12 NKJV).

—Gail Johnson, *Waurika, Oklahoma*

a garden of plants from the Bible

❀ Dozens of plants are mentioned in the Bible. Study them, then create a garden of as many species as you can that grow in your area.

❀ Print the plant name and the Bible reference on wooden stakes or garden markers to identify each plant.

❀ Make a desert garden in an old aquarium by layering sand and planting the desert plants of the Bible. Check the library or a nature store for books about watering, feeding, and caring for desert plants.

❀ Look for plants of the Bible in a local park or a botanical garden in your area with your family.

animals of the Bible

1 Make a scrapbook of cutout pictures, drawings, and photographs of all the animals you can find mentioned in the Bible.

2 Write a description of each animal's diet, habits, and habitat, and add a paragraph about how this animal is used in the Scriptures.

3 List the occasions and references you find.

4 What did you learn about this animal's ways and characteristics from the Bible? What was God trying to teach us by mentioning this animal in the Scripture?

a fishy story

How many times can you find fish or other creatures of the sea mentioned in the Bible?

Remember that a Bible word for whale was *leviathan*. Try looking up that word in a good concordance to find other references to the huge animals of the sea. (See Job 41:1–8, and Psalms 104:26.)

How has God used His aquatic animals to teach us important lessons? What can your family do to help God's water creatures and the environment they need for survival? (See Jonah 1:17; John 6:1–13; Matthew 4:19, 14:13–21, 15:32–39, and 17:24–27; John 21:4-6, and 21:10-13.)

Make a poster of the ways human beings are hurting or helping to guarantee the survival of water and the creatures God made to live in it.

the animals cooperate

There are many instances in the Bible of animals helping God accomplish His purpose. Sometimes creation and nature are more immediately responsive to the laws of God than human beings are.

The tents of robbers are not bothered, and those who make God angry are safe. They have their god in their pocket. But ask the animals, and they will teach you, or ask the birds of the air, and they will tell you. Speak to the earth, and it will teach you, or let the fish of the sea tell you. Every one of these knows that the hand of the LORD has done this. The life of every creature and the breath of all people are in God's hand (Job 12:6–10).

In your family worship time this month study the stories of the Bible in which God used animals, either directly or as examples, to teach human beings some eternal lesson.

Here are some examples:

- Balaam and the donkey—Numbers 22
- Daniel and the lions—Daniel 6
- Noah and the raven and dove—Genesis 8
- Elijah and the raven—1 Kings 17
- Jesus and the Passover donkey—Matthew 21
- Abraham, Isaac and the ram—Genesis 22:13
- the cock who crowed for Peter—Matthew 26:34
- the healing serpent in the wilderness—Numbers 21:1-9
- the whale that swallowed Jonah—Jonah 1
- the dog who ministered by licking Lazarus's sores—Luke 16:21
- the pigs who gave their lives to save the men from demon possession—Matthew 8:28-34
- the fatted calf who gave his life to celebrate the prodigal son's return—Luke 15:27
- all sacrificial lambs, cattle, doves, bulls—Leviticus 4:3
- the worm that taught Jonah a lesson—Jonah 4:7
- the eagle, symbol of strength—Isaiah 40:31
- the ant, symbol of industry and hard work—Proverbs 6:6
- the fish, feeding of five thousand—Matthew 14:17

As a family, make a scrapbook of all the animals that you study together and write on the page how God used that creature to accomplish His task on earth.

resolving conflict

Families are made up of many different personalities and temperaments, so it is inevitable that there will be disagreements and conflict from time to time. Having conflict is natural, but God's Word tells us many ways to resolve conflict without hurting each other.

Here is a list of suggestions for each person in the family:

💜 Take family worship time for several days to discuss these points. Locate, read aloud, and discuss each applicable Scripture verse.

💜 Post a copy of the list and references on the refrigerator, kitchen bulletin board, or other well-trafficked spot in your home.

💜 Pray for yourself and for each member of your family that God's spirit will knit you together with strong ties of love.

💜 Commit to each other to resolve conflict, and vow that you will value each other and stay together. Acknowledge that there will always be disagreement as long as there are people with personalities but that you believe problems can be resolved because you treasure your relationships more than having your own way.

resolving conflict

Constructive Conflict

- Seek peace, resolution, and reconciliation; Matt. 5:9; Eph. 4:5.

- Use Words "seasoned with grace" Col. 4:6, Eph. 4:29.

- Be "quick to listen" James 1:19.

- Show healthy, appropriate anger and the passion of involvement and commitment Eph. 4:26; Prov. 16:32.

- Stay focused on the issue at hand.

- Talk about your feelings in response to the conflict or breach in relationship. Be sure to use the personal pronoun "I" more than "you".

- Go in the attitude of humility, grace, mercy, and gentleness." Your greatest criticism is at the cross" Gal. 6:1–2.

- Know that some conflicts will take a long time to resolve. "Hang tough and tender" even if you have to love from afar for a season. Guard your heart and your tongue.

Destructive Conflict

- Seek victory, vindication, and vengeance.

- Have concern for the power of words Prov. 18:21; Gal. 5:15.

- Be "quick to speak", interrupt, explain, attack, and defend.

- Show disproportionate or destructive anger or passive hostility to protect yourself and to stay in control Eccl. 7:9; Prov. 14:17.

- Rehearse the history of every related and unrelated incident.

- Talk about the other person's faults and failures. Be sure to use the words "always" and "never" as much as you can.

- Go in the attitude of self-righteousness, power, blame, and shame. "If you lose, you die" 2 Cor. 12:20.

- If you don't win, bail out, move on. Someone, somewhere will agree with you and like you. Grow bitter and gossip as much as you can Heb. 12:14–15.

—Thanks to Scotty Smith of Nashville, Tennesee, for the use of these suggestions.

teachable moments

Scriptural Discipline

When my daughter, Elspeth, was four years old, she had a very independent attitude when it came to dressing herself. This seemed to be our only source of parent-child conflict. During this time I attended a series of lectures on discipline given by a layman in our church. At one of the lectures he encouraged parents to back up their discipline with Scripture. He explained that it was important to let children understand that discipline is part of God's wisdom for us.

I took note of this idea and decided to use it during our next "clothes conflict." At age four Elspeth already knew a lot of Scripture. I was convinced that she would have more respect for my authority and discipline if I backed it up with God's Word.

The next afternoon Elspeth went into a tantrum and insisted she knew how to tie her bow on the back of her dress. Since Mother knows best, I firmly turned her around and began to tie the bow myself. I explained to her that it was a good thing to ask for help. I told Elspeth that the Bible says, "Two are better than one."* At that remark Elspeth flung herself around, put her hands on her hips, and said, "Well, I can do all things through Christ who 'strengths' me!"**

I had to bite my lip to keep from laughing, but I realized I would always have to be one step ahead of my child when it came to applying the Scripture in her life and in my own!

—Cindy Merchant, Powhatan, VA

*Ecclesiastes 4:9 (NKJV)
**Philippians 4:13 (NKJV)

The LORD our God is the only LORD.
Love the LORD your God
with all your heart, all your soul,
and all your strength.

Deuteronomy 6:4–5

There is something built into our very beings that needs to worship.

We all have a deep sense that we are limited but that a Power

exists that is greater and bigger than we are. This inner feeling

makes worship a very important part of our lives.

But it is just as important for us to worship the right thing. When we

worship things or other people or our accomplishments or

even nature, our lives get all mixed up. Only God is worthy of our

worship. When we make a god of anything else, the result can be tragic.

Worship should be a part of every single day so that the rest of that

day can be kept in right relationship to the one Lord of our lives.

Let's worship! And worship the only One worthy

of our reverence, praise, and homage.

Section 5

let's worship together

Worship should be alive! It should be viewed as a necessary part of our lives. Keep it varied.

Family worship should include: (1) prayer, (2) Scripture, and (3) some bridge-builder from Scripture to life such as a story, drama, song, object lesson, poem, or devotional thought.

💜 **Play a song from a favorite children's recording** or (for older kids) a contemporary Christian artist or band. Then talk about the song and its Scripture base with the family.

💜 ***Read together*** a chapter from some Christian fiction like the C. S. Lewis *Chronicles of Narnia* series, Janette Oke books, or Dorothy Hamilton books. Also try, books like Corrie ten Boom's *The Hiding Place*, Walter Wangerin's *Ragman*, *Christy* by Catherine Marshall, or David Wilkerson's *The Cross and the Switchblade.*

💜 ***Use a Christian music video*** and discuss biblical mandates.

💜 ***Play a videotape*** of animated Bible stories after reading the passage illustrated from the Bible.

💜 Have family members (grandparents and young children too) ***take turns planning and leading*** the family worship time.

💜 ***Use instrumentalists*** in the family (playing piano, trumpet, autoharp, flute, guitar, drums) to enhance family singing of hymns, choruses, and gospel songs as well as contemporary praise songs and old favorite Sunday school songs.

💜 ***Have a slate or blackboard on which to write current prayer concerns.*** Whenever it comes to mind anyone in the family can write a request to be included at prayer times.

💜 ***Keep a family journal of prayer requests.*** Read back over former concerns occasionally to refresh your memory of ongoing concerns and to give thanks for answers and solutions that have come.

Vary the place of family devotions. Here are some suggestions:

✴ Sit in the middle of someone's bed for worship (take turns visiting each person's room).

✴ As night falls gather in pajamas and robes in the yard or around the porch swing.

✴ Meet around the fireplace in winter for warmth and togetherness.

✴ Pray around the breakfast table before school to save time and to prepare everyone for the day.

✴ Have worship around the campfire on camping trips or on family picnics in a state park.

✴ Take cushions to an upstairs deck or rooftop and locate the constellations, the moon, and the bright planets in view. Thank God for the lights that "rule the night."

chenille praise posture

God is an awesome God. When we come into His presence it affects us—our speech, our habits, our attitudes, and our body language. The Bible mentions several physical postures in relation to worship and praise. Look up the references listed below and read the verses as a family. From a craft store purchase a package of chenille-covered wires (pipe cleaners) in bright colors. Give several to each person and have fun making stick-people positioned in each posture of praise. Make a display. You may want to bend feet for your characters and glue them to a large piece of poster board. Write the verse beside each character.

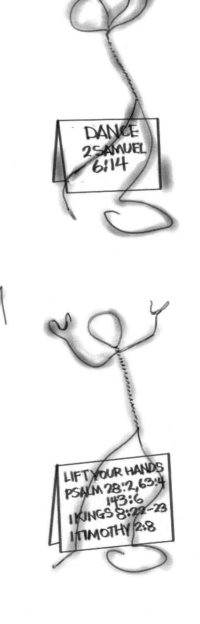

DANCE
2 SAMUEL
6:14

KNEEL:
PSALMS 95:6
LUKE 22:41

CLAP YOUR
HANDS
JOSHUA 5:14
MATTHEW 26:39
PSALM 47:1

STAND:
PSALM 33:8 (KJV)
1 KINGS 8:22

FALL ON YOUR
FACE
NUMBERS 16:22

BOW:
REVELATION 19:4
EPHESIANS 3:14

LIFT YOUR HANDS
PSALM 28:2, 63:4
143:6
1 KINGS 8:22-23
1 TIMOTHY 2:8

Most mothers of newborn babies are so busy and exhausted it's hard to have time to read God's Word or get time alone for personal devotions. While you are nursing your baby, read aloud softly whatever Bible passage you choose for the day. The baby will be comforted by your soft, familiar voice and will sense in it your love for him or her and for the words. *You* will be encouraged and energized by the power of the Word. Together you will feel the bond of God's love and protection. By the time the baby can begin to understand the words, you will have made him or her familiar with many passages from the Bible.

love, babies, and God's Word

a mother's prayer

Patricia W. Payton, a mother from Harahan, Louisiana, wrote this special prayer for her family. Your family may want to use it too.

Lord, I place my children under Your protection.
Place within their hearts a desire for You.
Keep them in Your care always.

Replace their thoughts with Your thoughts.
Replace their feelings with Your feelings.
Replace their desires with Your desires.
Replace their love for themselves, with Your love for them.
Enable them to really feel loved.
Replace their love for others with Your love for all.

Give them the grace to know that they are a temple of the Holy Spirit and that they should act accordingly.
Send them Your Holy Spirit with Your gifts of wisdom, knowledge, counsel, and understanding.
Be their constant companion in their joys and sorrows, and in their successes and failures.
Never let them be separated from You and never let the truth about You be kept from them.

Protect them from anything that is not from God.
Anoint them, mark them as Your own, and bring them into eternity with You.
I ask all this in the precious name of Jesus. Amen.

Many mothers in the Bible dedicated their children to God when they were very young, some even before the babies were born.
Hannah and Samuel—1 Samuel 1: 1–24
Sarah and Isaac—Genesis 21:1–8, 12
Elizabeth and John the Baptist–Luke chapter 1
Mary and Jesus–Luke chapter 1
The mother and grandmother of Timothy— 2 Timothy 1:5–6
Your family may want to have a special worship time dedicating your new baby to God. You may also want to publicly dedicate your baby to God at church. The next two pages contain a dedication worship service to be used at home and at church. Remember, each person in the family is dedicating himself or herself to God, too, to be an example, an encourager, and a fellow pilgrim for this child.

When a new baby is born into your family, you will want to dedicate the child to God and dedicate the whole family to raising and teaching him or her. Here is a dedication and worship service you may want to do at church or with a group of other close families at home.

welcoming a child

♥ The child's parents:

Lord, You have trusted us with one of Your priceless treasures, a human child. You have allowed us to share with You in the miracle of creation, and now that miracle has become flesh—we hold it in our arms. We are excited and full of joy! But we are also fearful. O Lord, we are imperfect parents in such an imperfect world. Speak to us. Assure us of Your nearness. Now, as we wait with this child, speak to us.

♥ Leader

(your pastor or a family mentor): Unless you are converted and become as little children, you will by no means enter into the kingdom of heaven. Whoever humbles himself as this little child, is the greatest in the kingdom of heaven. And whoever receives one little child like this in My name receives Me.[1]

♥ Choir

(or group of adult friends): Train up a child in the way he should go: and when he is old, he will not depart from it.[2] I am the way, the truth, and the life.[3]

♥ The whole congregation

(or all who are present at the dedication): Trust in the LORD with all your heart, and lean not on your own understanding. In all your ways acknowledge Him, and He shall direct your paths.[5]

♥ Leader:

And all thy children shall be taught of the LORD; and great shall be the peace of thy children.[4]

♥ Choir

(or adults): Cast all your cares upon Him for He cares for you.

♥ Prayer by layperson or a friend of the family:

Lord, we have here in our church family a new child, a new person, a new soul. The responsibility for this little person is too much for any two parents alone. They need the loving support of the fellowship of believers as they train and guide and nurture little (name). We give ourselves today, Lord, to the task. We accept the responsibility of helping to bring (name) to maturity in You. We will uphold him/her with our love, teach him/her the Word of God, encourage him/her when he/she fails, and we will be careful not to bruise this tender bud by harsh words, quick judgments, and cruel criticism. For truly, Father, this is our child, and we want to protect and teach him/her and to bring him/her to the moment when he/she will choose for himself/herself to know You as Savior and Lord of his/her life. Amen.

—*Gloria Gaither*

[1] Matthew 18: 3–4 (NKJV)
[2] Proverbs 22:6 (KJV)
[3] John 14:6 (NKJV)
[4] Isaiah 54:13 (NKJV)
[5] Proverbs 3:5 (NKJV)

Invite as many as possible of your extended family members—grandparents, aunts, uncles, cousins—especially those who have committed their owns lives to God. If you do not have believers in your family—invite close friends from the Family of God.

Prepare a small container (a tiny silver or crystal bowl, toothpick holder, small bud vase, etc.) filled with pure olive oil.

Cover a small table with a pretty cloth and place on it a children's Bible (to be signed and then given to the child later), a small vase of flowers (lilies of the valley, roses, or a single lily), and the small container of oil.

committing a child to God

♥ **Ask the father or mother, grandmother or grandfather** to read several of the "Promises to Parents and Children" in chapter 14. The father then might say: *It is the most awesome thing in our lives to realize that God has entrusted into our care the training of a tiny life, the molding of an eternal soul. This is a job too great for any two people alone. We need the wisdom of God and the help of all of you. This child needs prayer and good, trustworthy models if he/she is ever going to make it to maturity without emotional injury and find God's purpose in her/his life.*

♥ **Mother**: *To have the blessing of God and the primary persons in (name)'s life is very important. We would like for each of you who would like to, to dip your finger in this pure oil and anoint our child and give your blessing for his/her little life by telling what you pray to God for him/her.*

♥ **Let others follow.** When all who wish to do so have blessed the child, call on someone to pray a benediction.

♥ **Father:** *I will be first (dips his finger and anoints the baby's forehead). I bless my child in Jesus' name. I pray that she/he will serve God all the days of her/his life and that I will be a model she/he can follow without pain.*

This would be a good time to sing, share refreshments, and enjoy being together around the baby.

teachable moments

Variety and Perseverance

I've worked with my children for several years now, and the main advice I can give is . . . variety and perseverance. When one method doesn't seem to be going smoothly, try another. When you're tired of routine, take a break. But keep coming back . . . hang in there. Persevere!

—*Cindy D. Eis, Flagstaff, Arizona*

I Am a Promise

Words by
William J. and Gloria Gaither

Music by
William J. Gaither

I am a pro-mise– I am a pos-si-bil-i-ty, I am a prom-ise with a
cap-i-tal "P." I am a great big bun-dle of po-ten-ti-al-i-ty.—
And I am learn-ing to hear God's voice,— and I am
try-in' to make the right choice;— I am a pro-mise to be—

2nd time to Coda

an-y-thing God wants me to be.— I can go an-y-where that He
wants me to go;— I can be an-y-thing that He wants me to be.—
I can know an-y-thing that He wants me to know;— I can say an-y-thing that He
wants me to say.— I can climb the high moun-tains. I can

D.S. al Coda

cross the wide sea; I'm a great big pro-mise you see! I am a

Coda

I am a pro-mise to be an-y-thing God wants me— to be.

Our families are part of the body of Christ. In fact, our relationship to each other as part of God's family is even more important than our relationship to each other in the human family—and will outlast it on into eternity.

God's Word tells us to build up the body of Christ by encouraging and defending each other in as many ways as we can. Here are some examples:

♥ Sing encouraging songs together (Col. 3:16). Find songs to sing together as a family (or sing along with recordings) that communicate how much we need each other and how valued each person is in the family. Here are a few songs for kids and grown-ups:

"You're Something Special"
"I Am a Promise"
"Kids Under Construction"
"Beautiful Feet"
"I'm So Glad I'm a Part of the Family of God"
"Getting Used to the Family"
"You're My Brother, You're My Sister"
"Friends Are Friends Forever"

♥ Be submissive to each other (take turns) in love and always be submissive to God (Eph. 5:21, James 4:7).

♥ Be willing and quick to forgive (Matt. 6:14, Phil. 2:5).

♥ Share what you have and do it cheerfully (2 Cor. 8:3–5, Matt.5:41).

♥ Be eager to believe the best (1 Cor. 13:6–7).

♥ Be willing and quick to ask forgiveness (Matt. 6:12, Ps. 51).

♥ Get together often and keep the lines of communication open (Acts 2:42).

♥ Be patient. People don't mature over night (1 Thess. 5:14).

building up one another in the Body of Christ

♥ Share the things that are bothering you and pray for each other (Gal. 6:2).

♥ Defend each other when someone criticizes or attacks with ugly words (1 Cor. 13:7).

♥ Encourage and confirm each other when someone fails or feel inadequate (Heb. 3:13).

♥ Remind each other of the sufficiency of God (1 and 2 Peter).

♥ Keep God first, ahead of each person's individual preferences or agendas. When Jesus wins, everybody wins (Phil. 2:1–4)!

♥ Choose marriage partners who are believers so that you start in agreement on the most important (and eternal) issues (2 Cor. 6:14–18, Prov. 31:10–31).

Kids Under Construction

Words by
Gloria Gaither
and Gary S. Paxton

Music by
William J. Gaither
and Gary S. Paxton

Kids un-der con-struc - tion– may-be the paint is still wet!

Kids un-der con-struc - tion– the Lord might not be fin-ished

yet. In the job of con-struc-tion, I'm not all a-lone; The

Build-er is work-ing with me. He's giv-en the blue-print, the

tools and the plans To build all He wants me to be. Oh,

Alternate verses:

I'm more than an accident without a cause;
I'm more than a body and brain.
God made me on purpose– I'm part of a plan;
He cares and He knows me by name.

Dear Jesus, please make us more patient and kind–
Help us to be more like You;
And make room for all other children of Yours
For they are still growing up, too.

The growing I do and what I become
Begins with the path that I take;
Now what I will be as I'm growing along
Depends on the choices I make.

When I came to Jesus, I meant what I said;
I promised to give Him my heart.
But that kind of promise is more than just words–
Beginning was only a start.

Bible story rap

1 Write a rap song using a Bible story you have read.

2 Type the script and make copies for each person in the family.

3 Practice a few times using the rhythm setting on a keyboard or by setting up a stomp-clap rhythm with your hands and feet.

4 Invite your grandparents to share your family worship time.

5 Read the Bible story as it appears in the Bible.

6 Perform the rap you've rehersed, having everyone keep rhythm by clapping or snapping along.

7 Talk about how the story relates to your family life.

8 Pray together.

Parable of the Talents

by Joy MacKenzie
(adapted from Matthew 25)

Leader:	**Chorus:**

Leader:

Once there was a rich man →→→ *A rich man, a rich man*
Who had many servants →→→→→ *Lots of servants*
And he went on a trip →→→→→→ *A trip, a trip,*
A long trip*?*
A long trip!

Yes, a long trip
A lonnnnnnnng trip
But before he left the gate →→→→ *Before he left the gate*
He called to his servants →→→→→ *Servants, servants*
And gave to each of three →→→→ *Juuust three*
Some money →→→→→→→→→→ *Ooowhee!! money?*
Yes, money →→→→→→→→→→ *Money! How much?*
Betcha a bunch . . .

Well, the first of the servants
Was a very bright fellow →→→→→ *Very, very*
Very, very bright

A real sharp guy
With his head on right
And lots of talent →→→→→→→→ *Lots of talent*
The best →→→→→→→→→→→→ *The best*
Better than the rest

Leader:

So to him he loaned
Five thousand dollars➤➤➤➤➤➤➤➤*Dollars?*
Dollars!➤➤➤➤➤➤➤➤➤➤➤➤ *Five thousand*
dollars!

To the second servant,
A bright gal too
He counted out dollars . . .
One thousand—two➤➤➤➤➤➤➤*One thousand,*
two thousand
That's amazing!

Chorus:

Solo:
To that poor lady
It was plumb hair-
raising!

And the third with less talent
But still on his toes
Got one thousand—
dollar sign

Leader:

One and three 0's➤➤➤➤➤➤➤➤*One thousand-dollar sign,*
One and three 0's
Sooo, what did they do?
Do you suppose
They bought fine jewels
Or invested in clothes?
Perhaps they bought stocks
Or cattle or gold
Or dusty antiques
A thousand years old

Well—the first man was wise➤ *A wise man, a wise man A*
worker➤➤➤➤➤➤➤➤➤➤➤ *No shirker*
A doer➤➤➤➤➤➤➤➤➤➤➤➤ *Get-to-er*
 He doubled his money➤➤➤➤➤ ***Doubled?***
Yes, Doubled!➤➤➤➤➤➤➤➤➤*He doubled his share*
Brought twice the amount
That was left in his care➤➤➤➤➤*The second*
The second

Chorus:

Leader:

The servant with two ➤➤➤➤➤

This planner . . . **this** thinker
Was a zealous gal who,
With careful investment
Multiplied hers by two ➤➤➤➤➤

No...a good head for business
An assignment well done . . .
But oh, what that third **bright** man
Did with his plot ➤➤➤➤➤➤➤

Are you ready???????
He hid it ➤➤➤➤➤➤➤➤➤
He did . . . he hid it ➤➤➤➤➤➤

Chorus:

What was her fortune?
What did she do?

A regular Einstein
Made two out of one

Oh-oh, here's one for
Ripley's
believe-it-or-not

He hid it?
He didn't
Oh, he couldn't
He wouldn't . . .

Leader:

Safe in the ground
Perhaps scared that
he'd lose it ➤➤➤➤➤➤➤➤➤➤➤➤➤
Or afraid he would fail
At increasing its value
And be sorely disgraced ➤➤➤➤➤➤

He buried his talent ➤➤➤➤➤➤➤➤
When the master returned
He had nothing to show ➤➤➤➤➤

He was fired—thrown out
His share taken away

Chorus:

Oh, heaven forbid it

Didn't use it, didn't use it

What a waste!
What a waste!
Oh no, oh no

Oh no, oh no
He buried his money
He wasted his time
He blew his potential
How dumb . . .
What a crime!

Leader:

It was added to that of the
man who repaid
The most, worked the hardest,
Had given his best ➤➤➤➤➤➤➤➤➤

Chorus:

*The most. . . the hardest
Had given his best*

What you do with the talent
That is the test ➤➤➤➤➤➤➤➤➤ The test?

*What you do with the
talent
that is the test*

The test ➤➤➤➤➤➤➤➤➤➤➤➤➤ *The test
The test
The test
The test
The test
The test*

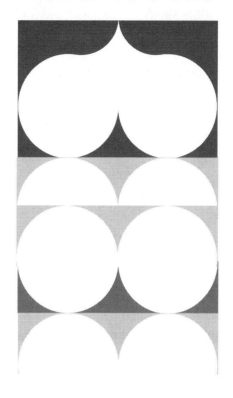

Many times the Bible speaks of fire as a symbol of God's presence and power. God's presence is one of love, not of fear or hate. To help your family remember that "perfect love drives out fear" (1 John 4:18), build a campfire and talk about its warmth and light. Talk about how fire is used to keep away animals, how it purifies, and how it consumes. The Word says that *God* is a consuming fire (Heb. 12:29).

fire and fear

1 Let each person in the family confess the things he or she fears most.

2 Collect a pile of sticks and give each stick the name of one of your fears.

3 Commit to give God each fear that creeps into your life from now on.

4 One by one, throw each stick into the fire; ask God to let His power and love consume each fear that troubles your life.

Here are some more verses to help keep you from being a victim of destructive fears. Remember that "fear (love, worship, respect) of the LORD is the begining of wisdom" (Prov. 1:7 KJV).

Ps. 23:4	Isa. 41:10
Ps. 27:1	Isa. 43:1
Ps. 34:4	Isa. 51:7
Ps. 46:2	Isa. 54:14
Ps. 76:7	Luke 12:5
Ps. 91:5	1 John 4:18

teachable moments

A Father's Quiet Time

"I did this as an example so that you should do as I have done for you" (John 13:15).

Peg Bedor, of Lapeer, Michigan, was a witness to the power of a father's example when she flew to Papua, New Guinea, to attend the funeral of her thirty-four-year-old son-in-law. David and his family had spent the previous four years planting churches in New Guinea. Following a morning run, he suffered a major heart attack that led to cardiac arrest, and David went to be with the Lord.

"My first morning there," shared Mrs. Bedor, "I noticed my grandson, seven-year-old Matthew, sitting on the couch reading his Bible. He looked up at me and said, 'My Daddy always had his quiet time; I will have mine.'"

A quiet example is a powerful way to help children hide God's Word in their hearts. It can help them make lifestyle choices that will strengthen their walk with the Lord forever.

What greater legacy could a young father leave to his son?

Always remember these commandments
I give you today. . .
talk about them.

Nothing makes us feel better about things than a good talk. Being

together is nice. Recreation such as a good ball game or a bicycle ride is fun.

But sooner or later there has to be time for a good talk with someone

who loves us and understands what we're going through.

We tend to talk about the things that really matter to us. It's important to

ask ourselves once in a while "What do I talk about most?" It's okay

to talk about great clothes or hairstyles or ball-game scores or the family

who moved in down the street. But if God is the center of our lives, our

conversations should show it; we should spend some

of our important talk on Him.

In this chapter we'll share some fun ways to talk about God's Word

and how it relates to all the other stuff we talk about.

Section 6 learning to talk about God

hot potato review

This game is great for reviewing Bible people, places, and things. Keep a Bible dictionary nearby to correct answers or to discover new Bible facts. Use a ball, a real potato, a pair of socks tightly rolled together, or an apple to play this game of hot potato.

1 The family sits in a circle on the floor.

2 The one with the "hot" potato calls out a Bible person, place, or event.

3 He or she quickly throws the potato to someone in the circle.

4 That person must give a short fact about the person, place, or event, then he or she tosses the potato to another player.

5 That person gives a short fact and throws it to another.

6 If a person cannot give a fact that has not been given, he or she is out of the round.

7 Or he or she can begin a new round by calling out a new person, place, or event.

Players will be surprised at how much they know about a Bible character, or sometimes they will be surprised at how little they know about a Bible place or event.

Children will listen harder at church to learn new facts so they can stump the family. The more often families play, the more they learn from each other.

Variation:

The first person tells the first part of a Bible story, then throws the potato to the next person, who then takes up the story where the first person left off. This continues until the whole story is completed. Example: The story of the birth of Christ, beginning with the angel's visit to Elizabeth, then Mary, etc.

Invite your friends (both adults and children) to a Bible masquerade party. On the invitation include the time and place and ask each person to dress like a Bible character and be prepared to tell who his or her character was in the Bible.

Bible masquerade party

Here are some ideas for your party:

Decorate with a biblical theme such as the streets of Jerusalem, the marketplace, a rooftop of a Holy Land house, the road from Jerusalem to Jericho, etc.

Serve food with biblical themes such as:

- manna
- loaves and fish
- grape punch (water on its way to wine)
- milk and honey (honeycakes or cookies)
- fruit salad made of fruit mentioned in the Bible: apples, pomegranates, grapes, etc.
- unleavened bread (pita bread)
- sandwiches with biblical meats and cheeses

Play biblical games

- Bible Trivia
- Name the Animal in the Story (on 3 x 5 cards type short scenarios of biblical stories related to animals. The person who is "it" draws a card and reads it; the others try to guess the animal in the story.)
- Bible charade
- Any of the other Bible guessing games found in this book
- Have a "guess who" time when each character gives hints as to who he or she might be. These can be a mixture of hints as to who he or she is in real life and in costume.

talk about telling the truth

God's Truth...

💜 Endures to all generations (Ps. 100:5)
💜 Reaches unto the clouds (Ps. 108:4)
💜 Came by Jesus Christ (John 1:17)
💜 Sets you free (John 8:31–32)

What is the opposite of the truth? A_____. God cannot tell a _____! One way we can be like God is to always tell the truth. It is not easy. The best way is to start when you are young. Telling the truth can become a good habit, and it will help you all your life. As you consider the importance of telling the truth, make a list describing:

💜 Times when it is especially hard to tell the truth.

💜 Times when a lie hurt someone you know.

💜 Times when you told the truth even when it was hard.

A SONG ABOUT TRUTH

Here is a fun song for the whole family to learn and practice. It is sung to the tune of "Give Me Oil in My Lamp."

"Give Me Truth"*

Give me truth in my youth; keep me honest.

Give me truth in my youth I pray.

Give me truth in my youth; keep me honest.

Keep me honest 'til I'm old and gray.

Tell the truth. Tell the truth.

Tell the truth at home, at school, at play.

Tell the truth. Tell the truth.

I will tell the truth each day!

* (by Dale VonSeggen. © Copyright 1979 One Way Street. Used by permission.)

path lights

If your family installs ground lights along a sidewalk, garden path, or driveway, take that opportunity to teach your children that "(God's) word is like a lamp for my feet and a light for my path" (Psalm 119:105).

1 Find a Scripture reference comparing God's word to a light for each light you are to install. You might even paint the reference neatly on each lamp.

2 When the lights are installed, wait until after dark to turn them on for the first time. Notice how dark the walkway is, how dangerous it might be to walk it with no light. Talk about what could happen if you were to walk along a path (such as our life's path) with no light on the way.

3 Turn on the switch and observe together what happens to the walkway, how it "appears" out of the darkness. Walk together in the new light.

4 Make a drawing of the walkway on a piece of poster board. From colored paper cut out path lights and write on each cut-out one of the "light" verses you found in the Bible.

5 As soon as you can recite one of the verses, glue the cut-out light to the path on your poster.

PSALM 119:109

II SAMUEL 22:29

Bible "light" quest—verses to memorize

1 Write or type each of these texts on a piece of yellow construction paper or 5" x 7" card. Cut each card in the shape of a heavenly light (star, moon, sun) or a fire flame.

A. How did we get light? (Gen. 1:3–5a)
B. What if I'm afraid? Who is my light? (Ps. 27:1)
C. How should I live? (Eph. 5:8)
D. What did Jesus say we are? (Matt. 5:14)
E. Who is the light of the world? (John 8:12)
F. Is the Word of God a light to me? (Ps. 119:105)
G. What is the fruit of the Spirit? (Gal. 5:22–23)

2 Learn the verse one phrase at a time. Go around the table each evening at suppertime, letting each person say the verse as far as he or she has learned it until that verse is completely learned by each person.

3 Repeat the learned verse, then add the first phrase of the next one, and so on, until all the verses are added to your family's memory bank.

4 Put seven bulky candles in a cluster on your table. Each time a verse is learned, light that candle for the evening meal until all seven are burning.

5 Tape the light cards to the refrigerator, the back door, or a bulletin board where you can be reminded of God's enduring light every day.

—taken, in part, from the *Kid Power Series* by Debbie Kennedy.

Tell Me a Story

Working mothers are not the only ones who suffer from lack of time with their children. Working grandmothers are often strapped for time, too, and many of them are not in their positions by choice. I am a grandmother; my husband has had a heart attack and triple-bypass surgery, and I am working outside our home. It grieves my heart not to be free to spend more time with our precious little grandchildren. I know God gave me the job, and that it was His perfect provision for our needs, but it is still a "praise-the-Lord-anyway" situation.

The Lord has led me to create stories for each of my grandchildren. I've given them the stories as gifts on special occasions. The ones for our two grandsons are told by the small, blue velveteen bear our son and daughter-in-law gave me for my birthday one year. A college student illustrates the stories for me. He is so talented that he has truly captured Blue Bear's sweet expression, and it has been such a joy to put the books together for Seth and Michael.

The books for the girls, ages three and five, are about angels. I want them to know they each have a guardian angel who is with them always. Through these stories I can share my faith with my grandchildren and they can read them anytime.

—Judy Lynn, Plano, Texas

talk about a miracle

Our God is a God of miracles! His very nature is to make the impossible possible. To appreciate who He is . . . keep your eyes open for daily miracles!

Exciting Old Testament Miracles
A bush that didn't burn (Exod. 3:1–4)
A sea crossed on dry ground (Exod. 14:21–31)
A donkey that talked (Num. 22:20–31)
A big wall that fell (Joshua 6)
A leper healed (2 Kings 5:1–19)
A cool fiery furnace (Dan. 3:8–30)

Mighty New Testament Miracles
A storm stands still (Luke 8:22–25)
A dead child lives (Matt. 9:18–20)
A hungry crowd is fed (John 6:1–14)
A blind man sees (John 9)

"I Spy". . . a Modern Miracle
To see a miracle, put on your "eyes of faith." Be watchful in the car, in the park, in a shopping mall, or at home. Search for the seemingly little things that demonstrate the nature of God. His Spirit at work in us is the greatest miracle of all.

💜 Make a family notebook of "I Spy" miracles. For example:

＊ I spy a flower growing up through a concrete sidewalk!

＊ I spy a man in a wheelchair with a smile on his face!

＊ I spy a foster parent loving a drug-addicted baby!

＊ I spy a job opening up for Dad since we prayed about a family move!

Now, think of some more miracles . . . Watch! They're all around you.

I Expect a Miracle

Words by
Gloria Gaither
and Reba Rambo

Music by
William J. Gaither
and Dony McGuire

Lyrics:

I an-ti-ci-pate— the in-ev-it-a-ble, su-per-nat—ur-al in-ter-ven-tion of God;— I ex-pect a mir-a-cle,— I ex-pect a mir-a-cle,— I ex-pect a mir-a- cle! To an-tic-i-pate:— to look for-ward to— what is like-ly to oc-cur;— In-ev-it-a-ble:— that cer-tain some-thing bound to hap—pen. Su-per-nat-ur-al:— the pow'r be-yond— all na-ture and— di-vine— Whose in-ter-ven—tion comes be-tween— me and my prob-lems just in time!— I an— cle! I ex-pect a mir-a-cle!

Teach them to your children . . .
When you sit at home.

Deuteronomy 6:7

Days when you end up staying at home—snowed-in days or rainy days or

sick days or "left-out" days, or times when your family is home in the evening

or on weekends—are good times for enriching your life with God's Word. In

this chapter we'll show you some fun ways to hide the Word in your heart

"when you sit at home."

Section 7

HIDING THE WORD on "at-home" days

teachable moments

Gramps Has a Story

I am a young grandfather (age fifty-eight) with seven grandchildren. One day while I was listening to the "Focus on the Family" radio program, they read a children's book titled *Ira Sleeps Over.** That was the beginning of a special character God led me to create called "Gramps." He wears red suspenders, a red bow tie, oval granny glasses, sleeve garters, and a variety of hats, and he walks with a cane!

Gramps loves to tell and read stories about Jesus and God's love to kids. He has performed at home for the grandkids, at church, and at neighborhood fairs. The story of Jonah comes alive to kids when Gramps puts on his captain's hat. I am excited about how this character helps spread God's Word in a new way.

—*James Micham, Rockville, Maryland*

*Bernard Waber, *Ira Sleeps Over* (New York: Houghton Mifflin, 1987).

If baseball cards are a hit with the young athletes in your home, start an after-school "Bible-Time Club." Include friends too. Barbra Kolk has five children, and four of them are boys. Her New Year's Resolution was to be daily in the Word of God with her children. She began an after-school "Bible-Time Club" at home and included the two neighborhood boys she watches each afternoon. They study the Gospels, and everyone wants to be "Jesus" in the role-play review. Here's how to start your own club:

baseball cards & the "Bible-time club"

1 Purchase a large pack of baseball cards.

2 Purchase a pack of 3 x 5 index cards.

3 Introduce and discuss an action story from the Gospels. Begin and end the story by reciting a key Bible verse related to the story.

4 Have everyone write the verse on a 3 x 5 cards.

5 Ask club members to carry the cards in their pockets and review the verse throughout the day.

6 By the next club meeting, if they have the verse memorized, they get two baseball cards for their collection.

7 Role-play the action stories from the Gospels, letting different kids play Jesus, the disciples, and other characters.

Barbra says she has benefited from this as much as the boys. While she teaches the Bible, they teach her about baseball.

when you sit at home... at the dinner table

Every night for a month have everyone in the family come to the dinner table with a verse about food or "the table." Before blessing the food, go around the table taking turns reciting the verses. Here are some examples:

Locusts: Matthew 3:4

Cheese: 1 Samuel 17:18, Job 10:10

Oil: Deuteronomy 12:17, Proverbs 21:20

Honey: Genesis 43:11, Judges 14:8

Bread: Genesis 18:6, Exodus 13:6, 1 Samuel 17:17, John 6:7

Vegetables: Numbers 11:5

Milk: Genesis 18:8, 1 Corinthians 9:7, Proverbs 30:33

Table: Exodus 25:23, Psalms 23:5(KJV), Acts 6:2

Butter: Deuteronomy 32:14, Proverbs 30:33

Raisins: 1 Samuel 25:18, 30:12

Fish: Matthew 7:10, Luke 24:42, John 21:9

Bible meals

Several special meals are mentioned in the Bible. Jesus often "broke bread" with His friends. Find as many references to Bible meals as you can, do some research in Bible dictionaries and study guides, then use your imagination and try to duplicate them, serving the food mentioned. Assign each person at your table a "character" who was present in the Bible meal. Act out the incident using the Scripture reference. Here are some suggestions:

The Last Supper (See Seder Supper, p. 121 for what was served at Passover.) (Luke 22:7–39; Mark 14:22)

The Feast of the Tabernacles (Leviticus 23:34–44)

The meal Jesus ate with the two persons on the road to Emmaus (Luke 24:13–35)

Elijah's two meals—one fed to him by ravens and one by a poor widow who experienced a miracle (1 Kings 17:1–24)

The hillside picnic of bread and fish served to five thousand people (John 6:9–13)

The meal of the rich man and poor Lazarus (Luke 16:19–21)

The feast given by the father for his prodigal son (Luke 15:11–32)

The fish dinner Jesus cooked on the beach (John 21:1–14)

The wedding feast in Cana where Jesus performed His first miracle (John 2:1–11)

Can you find references to other Bible meals?

what is Passover?

God commanded His people in Exodus 12 to observe Passover, the celebration of God's delivering His people out of the slavery of Pharaoh. The word *passover* comes from the night of the worst plague God sent to Egypt because Pharaoh, the Egyptian ruler, would not let the people go free. (Read about the plagues in Exodus 7–12.)

On that night God promised He would visit every house to execute judgment and would take the life of the firstborn son unless that family had marked the door of their house with the blood of a perfect lamb. If a family obeyed God and marked its doors, He would "pass over" that house, and no one in that family would die.

This plague finally convinced Pharaoh to let God's people go. Even to this day Jewish families and many Christian families celebrate the feast of Passover, as God instructed. Jesus and His disciples were Israelites, and it was this celebration that He shared with His disciples as His last supper with them. All Christians celebrate Communion—the breaking of bread and sharing of the cup of wine—because at the Last Supper Jesus instructed His followers to remember Him in this way.

At the Passover meal the father or grandfather is seated at the head of the table. The dishes to be served should be arranged where the father can pass them to the family.

As the meal progresses the youngest son asks the father or grandfather the following question four different times: "Why is this night different from all other nights?"

The first time the son asks the question, the father answers as he serves the unleavened bread: "For on other nights we eat bread, but tonight we eat only *matzoth*." Then he explains the meaning of the bread (see page 121).

The second time the father answers: "For on other nights we eat other vegetables, but tonight we eat only bitter herbs." He serves the *maror* and then explains the reason.

The third time the father answers the son's question this way: "For on other nights we do not dip our vegetables even once; but tonight—we dip twice." Salt water is then passed, and the father explains that it represents tears of sorrow. Parsley represents the new life possible. Next, the family dips the bitter herbs in *haroseth*, which sweetens the bitterness of the herb and reminds them that the sacrifice was sweetened by freedom. The color of the *haroseth* is a reminder of the mortar the Hebrew slaves had to use to erect buildings for their masters.

A fourth time the youngest son asks the ritual question, to which his father answers: "For on all other nights we eat sitting up, but tonight we all recline." Then he explains that in the old days free men sat on soft chairs or on couches, but servants had to stand before their masters or, while eating, sit on a hard bench. "Tonight, we celebrate our deliverance and freedom, so we sit in comfort and enjoy our freedom, wishing the same for all people."

This meal should end for Christians with the explanation that we are all "chosen people" who were born into God's family by believing in His Son, Jesus, our Messiah. As God's people, then, we should share the cup of joy with others out of gratitude that Jesus became the final Lamb to be sacrificed in order that our joy may be full.

The Passover Meal (Seder)

Passover lasts seven or eight days and begins with a meal and worship service Jewish families call *Seder*, meaning "order," because they always observe the celebration in a certain order. This first meal is made up of specific foods; each food has a special meaning.

To celebrate Seder you would serve:

Matzoth—wafers of unleavened bread. (It can be purchased from a Jewish delicatessen or from some grocers.) This is to remind us of the fact that the Israelites did not have time to wait for yeast bread to rise because they had to be ready to move when God said. For Christians, this reminds us also to live so that we are always ready to go when Jesus returns. Also, yeast sometimes represented the evil in the world. In contrast, God wants His people to be pure.

Maror—bitter herbs, usually freshly grated horseradish or other bitter, pungent vegetables such as onion. These herbs are a reminder of the Jews' bitter suffering in Egyptian slavery. This also reminds us that many have suffered that we may know the joy of the Good News of Jesus; so in our celebration, we remember the great cost.

Haroseth—a mixture of chopped apples, nuts, cinnamon, and wine. This represents the mortar with which the Israelites were forced to make bricks to build Pharaoh's great cities. (See Exodus 2:11–14 and 5:4–23.)

The shank bone of a lamb—a symbol of the lamb that was sacrificed for sins. To Christians, this represents Jesus, God's own gift of a perfect Lamb for the sins of all.

A roasted egg—an egg hard-boiled in the shell, to symbolize the free-will offering that was given with the lamb. This represents giving more to God than just what is demanded. This is a gift of love. Jesus was God's ultimate gift. God's law demanded only justice, but with the gift of Jesus, God gave us more than justice; He gave us mercy, love, and forgiveness.

Parsley or watercress—these two plants stay green the year around and represent the continual rebirth of growing things. To Christians, this represents God's gift of everlasting life because of the resurrection.

Wine or grape juice—representing joy. As the service proceeds, as each plague is mentioned, each person sips a little of the wine. This means that until total liberation, joy was incomplete. Jesus said at the Last Supper that the wine represented His own life's blood, poured out for us. He meant that He must die so that we could know the total joy of freedom and forgiveness.

Elijah's cup—in the center of the table is a goblet of wine that represents Elijah, whom the Israelites believed would foretell the coming of the Messiah. This cup is full to welcome Elijah and his announcement of the Messiah's return. Christians believe that John the Baptist was this "Elijah." (Jesus said in Matthew 11:14 that if the people could understand what was happening, they would recognize John as the promised Elijah who was to announce the Messiah's coming.) For Christians, this cup does not remain untouched, but is shared by everyone at the table in the joy that our hope has come true. The Messiah has come to us and is alive to give our lives eternal joy.

There comes a time in family life when it seems everyone goes off in a different direction. Young children often go to day-care or nursery school. Grade-school kids go to their various schoolrooms. Teenagers not only have their various schools but also places for many activities, such as rehearsal halls, gyms, or playing fields, as well as many interests in jobs, clubs, and sports. Parents leave for their places of work and spend a lot of time in their cars or on trains or busses getting there. Wouldn't it be great to remember each person at his or her workplace in your prayers each day?

"The LORD will watch over your coming and going both now and forevermore" (Ps. 121:8 NIV).

coming and going

Make a Photo-Cube Prayer Reminder

3 Purchase a square photo cube from a variety or photo store to display the pictures in.

4 Arrange the pictures in the cube. On a stick-on note write a promise from God's Word, chosen by each person, to put on his or her photo (see the list below).

5 Choose one side of the photo cube to focus on in family prayer at the table each day. Select a different "site" to pray for each day.

1 Create a colorful photo cube as a prayer reminder for your table. Everybody gets to help!

2 Plan a photo trip to the places where your family goes every day. Take a picture of each place.

- parks
- school
- workplace
- rehearsal
- subway
- car
- bus stop
- daycare center
- sports areas

God's Promises to Be with Us

Matthew 28:20
Luke 10:9
1 Corinthians 10:13
2 Corinthians 2:14
Philippians 4:19
James 4:8

who-said-it? bingo

1 Make bingo cards with five squares across and five squares down. Draw a Bible in the "free square" in the center.

2 In each square write the name of a Bible character. Use a Bible dictionary or index in the back of your Bible.

3 Give each player a handful of beans, buttons, or pennies to use as markers.

4 Take turns going around the table clockwise, each person giving a quote from a Bible character (it can be paraphrased), then asking, "Who said it?" The person then chooses someone to answer the question. If the person knows the answer, he or she may cover that square on his or her card.

5 Variation: A game leader can make a list of quotes from Bible characters and read a different quote each time.

Any player can raise a hand to answer.

Whoever has that name on his or her card can cover the square.

Players win when they cover one row of squares—down, across, or diagonally.

WHO SAID IT?-BINGO				
DANIEL	MOSES	SAMSON	ELISHA	NEHEMIAH
JOSEPH	PAUL	JOHN	ABRAHAM	NAOMI
ISAIAH	JEREMIAH	📖	JOB	ESTHER
SAMUEL	JOSHUA	SAUL	DAVID	ADAM
PETER	JAMES	MARY	RUTH	CALEB

Samples of paraphrased quotes for Who-Said-It? Bingo:

1. "Are you absolutely sure there is no room in the inn?" (See Luke 2:7.)
2. "I said it is definitely time to get on board! Don't push—two at a time." (Genesis chapters 6–7)
3. "The seventh time around is a charm, they say." (Joshua 6:1–14)
4. "I want to do good, but every time I try, I just mess up." (See Romans 7:15.)
5. "Yes, let those children come right over here and see Me." (See Matthew 10:14 and 19:14.)

"AT THE TABLE"

the good seed

"The good seed stands for the sons of the kingdom" (Matt. 13:38 NIV).

Think of all the things you eat every day that begin as a seed. Make a list of as many as you can. The seeds are easy to see in foods such as: apples, peaches, oranges, watermelons, etc. Other foods come from seeds that are unseen, such as flour and some vegetables: radishes, carrots, lettuce, etc. Seeds are an important part of God's plan for growing food.

The Bible tells us a lot about seeds, not only seeds that grow into food for us to eat, but also seeds that can be planted in our hearts—seeds of GOOD and seeds of EVIL. God's Spirit helps good seeds grow and helps us recognize evil seeds so they won't grow in us.

Growing Good Seeds

Create the following object lesson and keep it on your kitchen table. Or let each member of the family make his or her own.

1 Save, clean, and decorate two juice or coffee cans. To decorate, glue a mosaic of seeds on the can or pictures of food cut out of magazines.

2 Fill one can with potting soil and plant a fast-sprouting seed such as a lima bean. Keep the soil moist and give it morning sun.

3 In the other can place strips of paper with Bible verses about many kinds of seeds (see list below). Each day read a verse and ask yourself these questions:
1. Is the seed good or evil?
2. Why is it good or evil?
3. How can it help me grow as a Christian?

4 Keep a growth chart for your plant and for you!

Bible verses that mention seeds:

Psalm 126:6
Isaiah 55:10–11
1 John 3:9 (NKJV)
1 Corinthians 3:6
Galatians 3:16 (KJV)

Ecclesiastes 11:4,6
Matthew 13:38
John 12:24
2 Corinthians 9:10
1 Peter 1:23 (KJV)

flannel-board stories

At a discount store or craft shop buy:
- ♥ an inexpensive cork-covered bulletin board
- ♥ a piece of blue felt large enough to cover your board
- ♥ a shorter piece of green felt the width of your board
- ♥ several other squares of different colors
- ♥ white or clear craft glue.

1 Cut the blue felt to exactly fit the cork area of your bulletin board, then glue it on.

2 Cut the green felt to fit the length of board at the bottom and part way up both sides. Then cut the top to look like grassy hills. (Do not glue.)

3 From the brown felt cut tree trunks and other objects such as paths, biblical-era buildings, walking staffs, walls, etc.

4 From the other colors cut clothing, animals, jars, a sun, moon, etc. Cut people from brown-, cream-, or flesh-colored felt.

5 Tell a Bible story. As you tell it "build" the scenery, characters, and props with your felt pieces.

6 When you're finished, you may want to turn out the lights and focus a color wheel on your flannel board. As the colors change, different parts of your story will "pop out" and come alive.

arrows and shields

"Use the shield of faith with which you can stop all the burning arrows of the Evil One" (Eph. 6:16).

1 MAKING ARROWS:

Give each person four craft sticks and a fine-tip marker. On each stick write a hurtful statement you have heard. Discuss these painful comments and how they make us feel.

2 MAKING SHIELDS:

- Make a shield from a large piece of cardboard (a pizza box lid works well), a poster board, or a round aluminum platter.
- Look up verses on faith in the Bible (see list below).
- Discuss how we use these verses in our lives.
- Write the verses on the shield or write them on brightly colored sticky notes and stick them to the shield.
- Hang the shield on a door or wall.

3 STANDING FIRM:

- Choose up sides to take turns shooting at the shield.
- Each side takes turns shooting the arrows by speaking the comments and then shooting the craft sticks with rubber bands toward the shield. As the "arrows" bounce off the shield, members of the other side recite the verses describing the power of faith. (Be sure to stand far away from the flying arrows!)
- Change sides, giving everyone a chance to play both parts.

4 Guided conversations:
- How did you feel when you were the shooter?
- How was it different when you were standing firm?
- How did others on your side help you?
- How can this game change the way you pray about painful comments or situations?

Examples of "faith" references
to start your search:
Matthew 17:20
Mark 11:22
Romans 1:17, 5:1,10:17

1 Corinthians 13:13
2 Corinthians 5:7
Hebrews chapter 11

Bible-celebrity "to tell the truth"

Invite your youth group, your Sunday school class, or two or three other families to your house to play "To Tell the Truth."

1 Put the names of several female Bible characters in one basket and male characters in another. Choose equal teams of males and females; the team that is "it" chooses a character of the same gender. The team members then go where nobody can hear them and choose one among them to be the person who will be the "real" biblical character. Then each person makes up a life's story, but only the "real" character will have <u>all</u> the facts straight.

2 The first team sits in chairs facing the rest of the players. One by one each person introduces himself or herself with the sentence, "My name is _____," using the biblical character's name. Then he or she tells his or her story.

3 The opposing team then asks questions addressed to the various players that can only be answered with yes or no. Only the "real" character answers all the questions truthfully.

4 The first player to gather enough "evidence" to correctly name the right character wins.

5 Then another team chooses a Bible character and takes its turn.

who turned the lights out?

Have you ever wondered how it would feel to be blind? Do you know anyone who is blind? If you don't know how it feels to be blind, you probably cannot fully appreciate the miracle Jesus did in John 9:10–12, when He healed a man who had been blind since birth. The man had never seen a sunrise or looked at his mom's smile. When he sat down to dinner, someone had to tell him what kind of food was on the table.

Extra Napkins All Around! **1**

When you set the table for dinner tonight, give everyone an extra napkin and a safety pin. Before you serve the meal help everyone blindfold themselves with the napkin. Explain that you are going to have dinner without using your sight, then give everyone a plate filled with food. Tell the family members instead of saying the usual, "thank You, God, for this food" prayer at the beginning of the meal, you will wait until the end of dinner. The prayers will surely be very different from your usual blessing!

2 After Dinner, Read John 9

Remove the blindfolds, and take turns reading parts of the story of Jesus' miracle.
Why was the man blind?
How did Jesus heal the man?
What did the man have to do to see?
Why did people doubt the miracle?

How about You?

Do miracles happen today? What miracles do you need Jesus to do for you? What do you need to do to receive His miracle? What are some miracles we have every day that we don't notice?

Pray for one another, giving thanks to God for your sight and for His miracles, especially the miracles we have in our everyday lives.

I Expect a Miracle

Words by
Gloria Gaither
and Reba Rambo

Music by
William J. Gaither
and Dony McGuire

I an- ti- ci- pate the in- ev- it- a- ble, su- per- nat- ur- al
in- ter- ven- tion of God; I ex- pect a mir- a- cle,

2nd time to Coda

I ex- pect a mir- a- cle, I ex- pect a mir- a-

cle! To an- tic- i- pate: to look for- ward to what is

like- ly to oc- cur; In- ev- it- a- ble: that cer- tain

some- thing bound to hap- pen. Su- per- nat- ur- al: the

pow'r be- yond all na- ture and di- vine Whose in- ter- ven- tion comes be- tween

D.S. al Coda

— me and my prob- lems just in time! I an–

⊕ Coda

cle! I ex- pect a mir- a- cle!

lyrics: Gloria Gaither and Reba Rambo   music: Bill Gaither and Dony McGuire

privilege and favor prizes

Instead of store-bought trinkets for prizes in family games and contests, give special privileges or favors.

Save the small containers film comes in or other small containers such as prescription-drug bottles with the labels removed, tiny baby-food jars, etc.

1 On strips of brightly colored construction paper write a special privilege or a promise by someone in the family to do a favor, signed by the contributor.

2 Roll strips around a pencil and secure them with a tiny piece of adhesive tape.

3 Place one privilege or favor in each container and seal its lid.

4 Use a pretty basket or decorated school box to store the containers.

5 When someone wins at Bible games or projects, let that person choose a prize from the basket or box.

I WILL WEED THE SIDE YARD

Examples:

You may stay up one extra hour on any weekend night you choose. *mom*

You may pick your favorite restaurant the next time we eat out. *Dad*

You may plan the next family outing. *BEN*

I will make your bed for you any one morning you choose. *SANDY*

I will take your turn at setting the table any Sunday you choose. *Tom*

I will wash your car or clean up your bicycle next Saturday. *Joey*

You may skip your next turn at doing dishes. *Marcy*

I will bake cookies the next time you have friends over. *mom*

Bible charades

1 Divide players into two teams.

2 Each team puts in a bowl the names of several Bible characters written on folded slips of paper.

3 Each team chooses a team member to be the timekeeper.

4 The first team chooses someone to be "it," and that person chooses a character from the other team's bowl and reads it silently, not letting anyone on his or her own team see.

5 "It" must then "act out" for his or her own team the character chosen without using props or speaking a single word while the other team keeps track of the exact number of seconds used, not to exceed three minutes. If "its" team takes more than three minutes to guess the character's name the team is credited with the full three minutes and must give the floor to the other team's "it."

6 Play as long as you wish. The team that finishes with the least amount of time used, wins.

I will build my church

You will need:
- ♥ a large piece of poster board
- ♥ a felt-tip marker
- ♥ scissors
- ♥ adhesive tape

1 On the poster board have the best artist you know draw a large church. The more detail the artist draws, the more fun you'll have. For instance, your artist might include building stones or blocks, windows, steeples, etc.

2 Cut out the church, then cut it in several pieces with the scissors. Put a piece of tape at the edge of each piece.

3 Give a piece to each person (or if there are enough pieces, each person might have two pieces).

♥ This game can also be played with two drawings and two teams who race to finish first.

4 On a flat surface, such as a door or smooth wall (or you could also use another big piece of poster board), try to "build" the church back into shape.

♥ Discuss what Peter said about our being "living stones" (1 Pet. 2:5) and what Jesus said about building His church (Matt. 16:18).

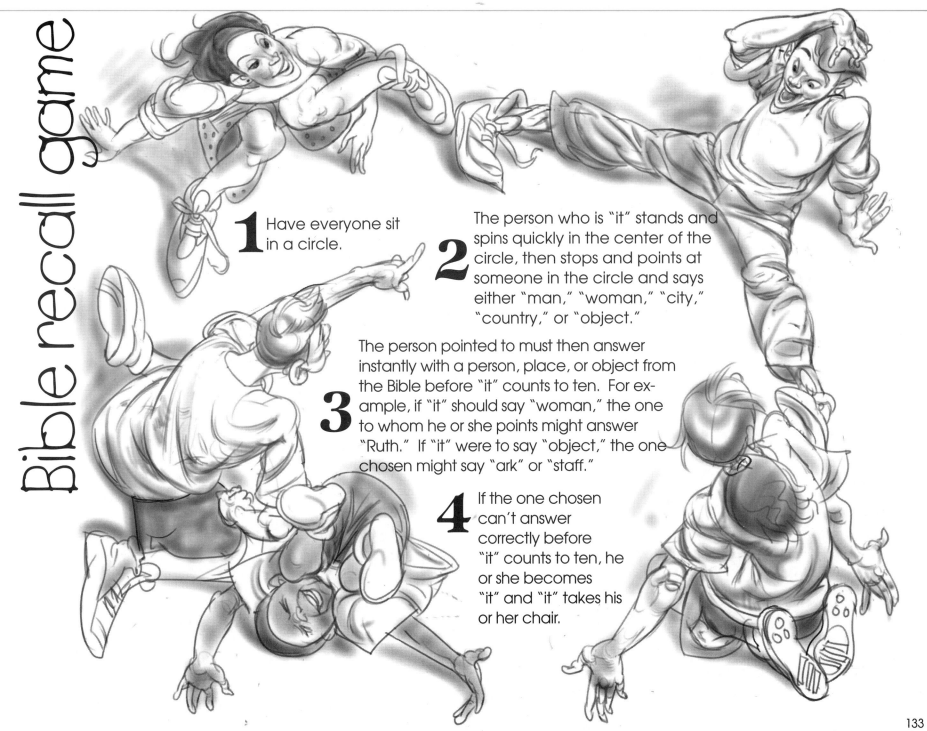

Bible recall game

1 Have everyone sit in a circle.

2 The person who is "it" stands and spins quickly in the center of the circle, then stops and points at someone in the circle and says either "man," "woman," "city," "country," or "object."

3 The person pointed to must then answer instantly with a person, place, or object from the Bible before "it" counts to ten. For example, if "it" should say "woman," the one to whom he or she points might answer "Ruth." If "it" were to say "object," the one chosen might say "ark" or "staff."

4 If the one chosen can't answer correctly before "it" counts to ten, he or she becomes "it" and "it" takes his or her chair.

Teach them to your children . . .
when you walk along the road.

Deuteronomy 6:7

Most of us are constantly on the move. We commute to work and to school. We take the bus or train into the city. We fly to Disneyland or to visit relatives or to the beach for a vacation. Travel time is a great time to "hide the Word."

Taking walks in the woods, climbing mountains, exploring caves, combing beaches—these are perfect opportunities to relate God's Word to our daily journey.

The next few pages are full of great ways to hide the Word when you are on the move.

HIDING THE WORD

Section **8**

Bible treasure hunt

There are many "valuables" mentioned in the Bible. Plan a "treasure hunt" using Bible references as clues.

1 Draw a map of your yard, orchard, field, or where you and your friends go to church, or maybe a relative's hillside.

2 Collect the treasures listed below and hide them in places that appear on your map. Put the appropriate Bible reference near the location on your map where a "treasure" might be found.

Here are some examples:

* a pearl   * a jewel
* a coin   * a crown
* gold coins   * a key
* silver coins   * rich spices (potpourri in a little box)
* a ruby   * a diamond (don't use a real one!)
* crystal   * purple cloth (a symbol of royalty)

3 Using your Bible concordance or Bible dictionary, find references for Bible objects you can use as clues on your map.

4 On your invitations ask each person invited to bring a Bible to look up clues.

5 Make copies of the map for each person on each team.

6 Give a signal to start and stop the hunt (like ringing a dinner bell or blowing a loud whistle).

7 When everyone comes back from the hunt, read each Scripture clue from the Bible and see who found that treasure. The person or team to find the most treasures wins.

8 Give a prize for the most treasure found. Some prize ideas are a new Bible board game, a Bible storybook, or a fun Bible activities book. Some other suggestions are in the Resources Section at the end of this book.

9 Serve refreshments. You might even want to serve "milk and honey" as a refreshment: Mix peanut butter with honey and whip it until it is smooth. Spread the mixture over homemade bread or graham crackers. You can use sharp cookie cutters to cut honey-bread sandwiches into seasonal shapes. Serve with colorful cups filled with ice-cold milk.

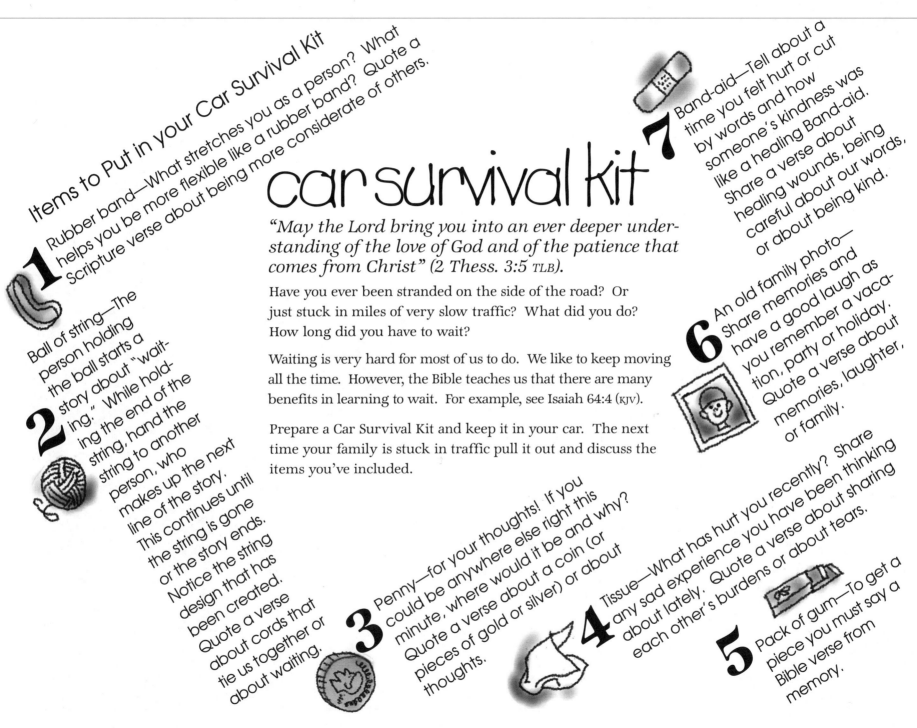

car survival kit

"May the Lord bring you into an ever deeper understanding of the love of God and of the patience that comes from Christ" (2 Thess. 3:5 TLB).

Have you ever been stranded on the side of the road? Or just stuck in miles of very slow traffic? What did you do? How long did you have to wait?

Waiting is very hard for most of us to do. We like to keep moving all the time. However, the Bible teaches us that there are many benefits in learning to wait. For example, see Isaiah 64:4 (KJV).

Prepare a Car Survival Kit and keep it in your car. The next time your family is stuck in traffic pull it out and discuss the items you've included.

Items to Put in your Car Survival Kit

1 Rubber band—What stretches you as a person? What helps you be more flexible like a rubber band? Quote a Scripture verse about being more considerate of others.

2 Ball of string—The person holding the ball starts a story about "waiting." While holding the end of the string, hand the string to another person, who makes up the next line of the story. This continues until the string is gone or the story ends. Notice the string design that has been created. Quote a verse about cords that tie us together or about waiting.

3 Penny—for your thoughts! If you could be anywhere else right this minute, where would it be and why? Quote a verse about a coin (or pieces of gold or silver) or about thoughts.

4 Tissue—What has hurt you recently? Share any sad experience you have been thinking about lately. Quote a verse about sharing each other's burdens or about tears.

5 Pack of gum—To get a piece you must say a Bible verse from memory.

6 An old family photo—Share memories and have a good laugh as you remember a vacation, party or holiday. Quote a verse about memories, laughter, or family.

7 Band-aid—Tell about a time you felt hurt or cut by words and how someone's kindness was like a healing Band-aid. Share a verse about healing wounds, being careful about our words, or about being kind.

learn to "see" what we see

In most parts of the country we can drive along the road and enjoy the beauty of the four seasons. God made such a beautiful world. A beloved American song says it this way:

O *beautiful for spacious skies, for amber*
waves of grain.
For purple mountain majesties above the
fruited plain.
America! America! God shed His grace on thee,
And crown thy good with brotherhood,
From sea to shining sea!

—Katharine Lee Bates
"America, the Beautiful"

When we are in the car, we are usually in a hurry to get where we are going. Our minds are on what we have to do. When was the last time you looked out the car window and really noticed God's wonderful nature? Jesus said, "*Look at the birds! They don't worry.*
Look at the field lilies! They don't worry" (paraphrase of Matt. 6:26–28).
The problem is, we do forget to *look* and we do worry!

After-School Walks

My father loved the Psalms. I can still quote Psalms I learned at the age of six or seven. After school each day I used to go to the nearby college science lab filled with mice and rats where my father worked. I would stay with him until he was ready to go home. We would walk home together, and on the way he would recite the Psalms. He would help me repeat them after him.

—*Mary Alice Kingsbury, Glen Gardner, New Jersey*

a sun-visor art car decor

To remind your family of the four seasons and of Jesus' instructions, create sun-visor pockets for your car.

1 Use a cloth tape measure to measure the width of the car's sun visors.

2 Cut a strip of butcher paper twice the size of each visor and tape the ends together to make a pocket that will slip around the visor. A brown lunch sack with the bottom cut off will also fit on most visors.

3 On the two visors you will now have four sides to decorate with beautiful scenes of spring, summer, fall, and winter. Or you may want to write Bible promises such as the words of Jesus in Matthew 6.

Rotate the pockets often and create new ones.

Grandparents might want a set for their car too!

parts are parts

Moving vehicles have many parts. It doesn't matter if you travel by car, plane, bus, bike, or train; they all have many parts, and every part is important. A good mechanic is usually needed to keep the parts running smoothly.

Families have parts too—and they are each very important. We need God to keep us running smoothly. When we understand each other, we will better appreciate how we work the Bible says we all have different abilities, but we are all part of one body (Rom. 12:4–6).

What is the most important part of a car? The tires? brakes? steering wheel? engine, horn? A car might run without lights at night, but would your family want to ride in it? Is one part more important than another, or are all the parts equally essential?

Who is the most important person in your family?
Think about all the different personalities in your family. Try to identify your family members with the parts of a car.

1 Draw a picture of your car.

3 Keep the drawing in the car as a prayer reminder.

2 Label the different parts of the car with a family member's name. Rejoice in each one's unique way of making your family run in "tiptop shape." Remember that if there is a breakdown, God's power can fix each part. Give thanks for how He has put you all together.

"So in Christ we who are many form one body, and each member belongs to all the others"
(Rom. 12:5 NIV).

Who is the steering wheel? **Who** gets others to go his or her way?

Who is the rearview mirror? **Who** usually sees things backward?

Who is the horn? **Who** talks the most?

Who is the tires? **Who** is always on the go?

Who is the brakes? **Who** tries to stop a problem before someone gets hurt?

Who is the glove compartment? **Whose** room needs cleaning?

Who is the engine? **Who** is the brains of the family?

Who is the pistons? **Who** is up and down the most?

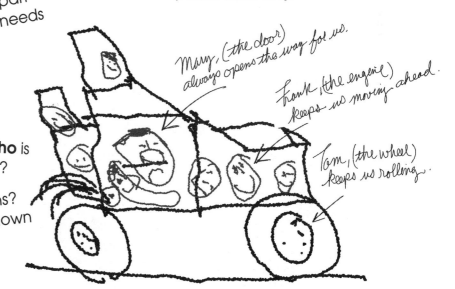

Mary, (the door) always opens the way for us.

Frank (the engine) keeps us moving ahead.

Tom, (the wheel) keeps us rolling.

angels at the wheel

While angels have many jobs to do, one of their most important is to protect us from danger.

The Angel of the Lord guards and rescues all who reverence him" (Ps. 34:7 TLB).

For he orders his angels to protect you wherever you go. They will steady you with their hands to keep you from stumbling against the rocks on the trail" (Ps. 91:11–12 TLB).

Before you start on a trip, it is a good idea to say a prayer asking God to send His angels to protect you and your family. We do not pray to angels, but we can thank God for His protecting angels. Angels have great power to do God's work.

Angels Protect God's Servants
> Exodus 23:20–33
> Daniel 6:16–23
> Acts 12:1–19
> Acts 27:13–44

If you should see an accident on your trip, stop and ask God to send His special angels to be with those who might be hurt.

ANGELS ARE WATCHING OVER ME
During your next car trip . . .

- Make angel cutouts from paper plates to hang on the rearview mirror.

- Draw angels on a road map in all the places you will visit.

- Make a family contest of creating the best bumper sticker to put on your car. Everyone gets to vote.

- Sing a song about angels. If you don't know one, make one up.

- Make bumper stickers illustrating a Bible verse about angels. (Use plain white contact paper.)

My Father's Angels

Words by
William J. and Gloria Gaither

Music by
Dony McGuire

CHORUS
They're all a-bove me, be-neath me, be-fore me— They're all a-round me; My Fa-ther's an-gels all pro-tect me ev-'ry-where.

They're all a-bove—

VERSE
1. I could nev-er stray—
2. E-ven when the night's—

— so far my Fa-ther would lose track of where I am;—
— so dark I just can't see a thing in front of me.

— An-gels walk be-side me, hold-ing tight-ly to my hand.— They're all a-bove—
— I won't need to wor-ry; They can see—

they see me. They're all a-bove me, be-neath—

— me, be-fore me— They're all a-round me; My Fa-ther's an-

gels all pro-tect me ev-'ry-where.

finish the verse

As you drive or ride in your car, choose one person in the family to think of a Bible verse you have learned.

The one who starts is "it." He or she recites the first phrase of the verse, then calls the name of another person. Before "it" can count to ten, the one named must finish the verse. If he or she can finish the verse, he or she gets to start the next verse and call on someone else.

If the person called can't finish the verse, he or she loses the turn and "it" may call on someone else and count to ten again.

When we travel along the roads and highways, signs give us instruction and warning. The Word of God gives us instructions and warnings, too, for the "road of life."

For every road sign you see, think of verses in the Bible that give you the same kind of direction. After you have learned several, have a race to see who in your car can be the first to think of a Scripture verse to match the signs you see.

road signs

To play the game:

Draw the road signs on a sheet of paper with boxes following each sign. Make copies for everyone in the car. As you travel, watch for the signs. Some you will see often; some you will see only once in a while.

When you see a sign, think of a Bible verse to match that warning or instruction. If you can recite it, make a check in one of the boxes by that sign.

The first person to check all the boxes gets to choose the restaurant for lunch or dinner—or even the destination for the next family trip!

Here are some examples of scriptural instructions similar to those of modern road signs. Keep in mind that the words may differ, but the meanings are basically the same.

U-Turn/Sharp turn/Curve

- "Turn us again, O God" (Ps. 80:3 KJV).
- "Turn us, O God of our salvation" (Ps. 85:4 KJV).
- "Turn you at my reproof" (Prov. 1:23 KJV).
- "Turn from evil ways" (Jer. 18:8).
- "Turn . . . to God" (Hos. 12:6 KJV).
- "Turn from foolishness" (Acts 14:15).

Stop

- Stop lying (Ps. 31:18 and 119:163 Prov. 6:17 and 12:22).
- Stop stealing (Exod. 20:15, Deut. 5:19 Matt. 19:18, Mark 10:19 Luke 18:20 and Eph. 4:28).
- Stop swearing (Exod. 20:7, Matt. 5:34 and James 5:12).
- Stop hurting children (Matt. 18:6 and Mark 9:42).
- Stop being immoral (Prov. 6:25 Matt. 5:28, 32; Rom. 1:24,13:14; Eph. 4:19).

Yield

- "Yield yourselves unto the Lord" (2 Chron. 30:8 KJV).
- "Yield to rulers" (Eccles. 10:4).
- "Yield to others to live in peace" (Rom. 12:18).
- "Yield to others in honor" (Rom. 12:10).
- "Yield to each other because of love" (Eph. 5:21).
- "Yield yourselves to God's authority" (James 4:7).
- "Yield to the authority of the government and national leaders for the Lord's sake" (1 Pet. 2:13).

Slow

- Be slow to get angry (Prov. 14:29, Neh. 9:17, Ps. 103:8 and 145:8).
- Be slow to talk back (James 1:19).

Think of other verses to go with more of the signs you see.

Hill

- "Ascend into the hill of the LORD" (Ps. 24:3 KJV).
- "Who shall dwell in thy holy hill?" (Ps. 15:1 KJV).
- "This is the hill which God desireth to dwell in" (Ps. 68:16 KJV).
- "Every . . . hill shall be made low" (Isa. 40:4, Luke 3:5).
- "A city that is built on a hill" (Matt. 5:14).

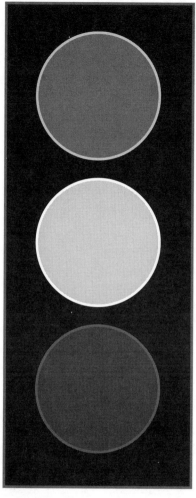

stoplight race

- Memorize verses from the Bible that instruct us to *stop*, use *caution*, and *go*.

- Whenever your family stops for a stoplight when traveling, try to call out as many verses as possible to match the light before it changes. Try to top your last total each time.

- When you pass other road signs, try to think of a related verse before you go by each sign.

- In your spare time find and learn new verses to use next time.

For example:

Go

"I will **go** in the strength of the Lord" (Ps. 71:16 KJV).
"Where can I **go** from your Spirit?" (Ps. 139:7 KJV).
"I . . . will **go** with you" (Exod. 33:14).
"**Go** ye therefore, and teach all nations" (Matt. 28:19 KJV).
"**Go** into all the world and preach the gospel to every creature" Mark 16:15 NKJV).
"Let my people **go**" (Exod. 5:1 and 7:16).
"Whither thou **goest**, I will **go**." Ruth 1:16 KJV).

Caution

"Beware of false prophets" (Matt. 7:15 KJV).
"Beware of men: for they will deliver you up to the councils, and they will scourge you in their synagogue" (Matt. 10:17 KJV).
"Beware of the leaven of the Pharisees" (Matt. 16:6 KJV).
"Looking diligently lest anyone fall short of the grace of God; lest any root of bitterness spring up to cause trouble, and by this many become defiled" (Heb. 12:15 NKJV).
"Beware of covetousness" (Luke 12:15 NKJV).

Stop
"If anyone is stealing, he must stop" (Eph. 4:28 TLB).
"Grieve not the holy Spirit" (Eph. 4:30 KJV).
"Let all bitterness and wrath and anger and clamor and evil speaking, be put away from you, with all malice" (Eph. 4:3 KJV).
"Stop lying to each other" (Eph. 4:25 TLB).
"Stop being mean, bad-tempered and angry. Quarreling, harsh words, and dislike of others should have no place in your lives" (Eph 4:31 TLB).
"Stop evaluating Christians by what the world thinks about them or by what they seem to be like on the outside" (2 Cor. 5:16 TLB).
"Let us stop going over the same old ground again and again, always teaching those first lessons about Christ. Let us go on instead to other things and become mature in our understanding, as strong Christians ought to be" (Heb. 6:1 TLB).
"Little children, let us stop just saying we love people; let us really love them, and show it by our actions" (1 John 3:18 TLB).

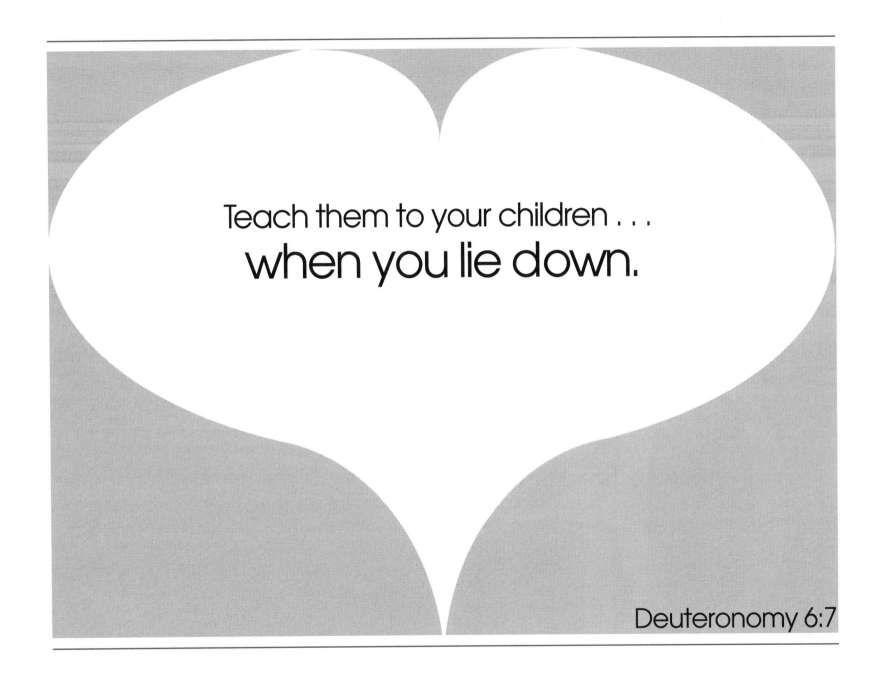

At the close of the day our minds are winding down and our bodies are

ready for rest. The Bible says that God "will keep him in perfect

peace, whose mind is stayed" on Him (Isa. 26:3 NKJV). Ideas and words

that are in our minds when we lie down for the night are likely to

stay with us as a part of our subconscious and when we

awaken again as a part of our conscious thought patterns.

If God's Word is to shape our lives, what better time could there be to

store it away than when we lie down?

In this chapter you will find some end-of-the-day and bedtime games and

activities to help you go to sleep thinking on the good things.

Section 9

bedtime ways to hide the Word

Fear is often related in some way to the unknown. Once we dare to look the fearful thing in the face, it isn't so scary anymore. It also helps to know that Someone we love knows about our fears and still loves us.

casting out fear

1 Gather as a family and go around your family circle telling some things that make you afraid when you go to bed at night. It may surprise the children to learn that fears stalk parents in the night too.

2 Pray about the things that make each of you feel afraid and commit them to God's keeping.

❤ Getting family priorities straight and trusting God to care for you when you put His Kingdom first. Read some of these verses together:

Luke 12:4–7
Luke 12:22–34
Matthew 19:24–31
Hebrew 13:1–6

3 Commit to pray for each other. Assure each other that you will be available to pray—even in the middle of the night—if someone wakes up afraid.

❤ When bad people seem to be winning; when you feel panicked about the wickedness around you: Psalm 55

❤ Learning that only Jesus can calm the storms of our lives: Matthew 8:23–27 Mark 4:35-41

❤ Learning that true love gets rid of fear: 1 John 4:7–12

❤ Trusting God to punish or carry out justice: Deuterononmy 32:35 Romans 12:19

❤ Encouraging each other, especially when you are feeling weak and shaky: Isaiah 35:3–10

bedtime thanksgiving

Praise and thanksgiving are the best ways to wrap up the day.

♥ Before you go to sleep, think of all the ways God has answered your prayer, helped you in difficult moments, or protected you and your family.

♥ List them in your journal or just speak them aloud to someone in your family. Express your thanks to God together and then go to sleep concentrating on the good things.

Here are some verses to help you give thanks together as a family:

- Hebrews 12:28
- 1 Chronicles 16:8
- Psalm 100
- 1 Corinthians 15:57
- 2 Corinthians 2:14 and 9:15
- 1 Thessalonians 5:18

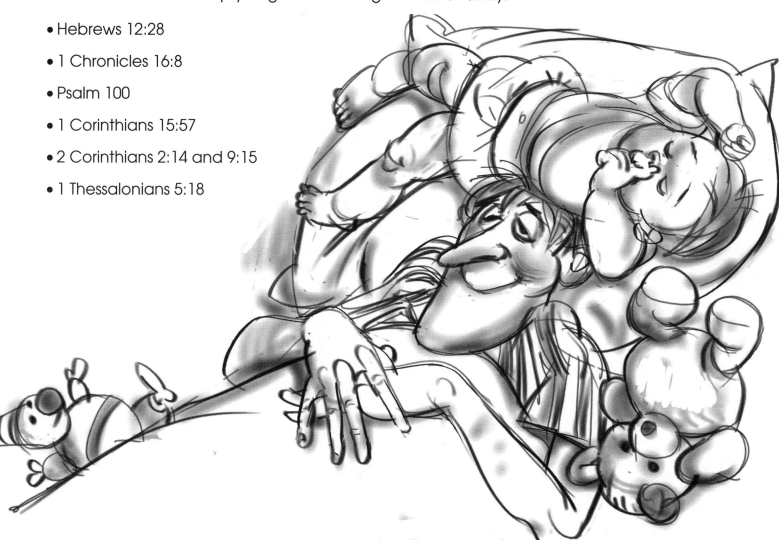

"God's covering" quilt

Make a quilt to remind you or your child (or grandchild) that we are covered by the protection and blessing of the heavenly Father as promised in His Word. Here are some suggestions for the quilt squares or pieces:

OBJECTS THAT ARE GIFTS OF GOD TO YOUR LIFE SUCH AS:

❤ the **sun**, **moon**, and **stars** (Ps. 19)

❤ the **rain**, clean **water** (Matt. 5: 45, Ezek. 34:26)

❤ the **season's** planting time and harvest
  (Eccl. 3:1, Gen. 8:22)

❤ **food** (Matt. 6:26, Luke 12:24)

❤ **shelter** (Ps. 61:1–5)

❤ **friendship** (Prov. 17:17, Prov. 18:24
  John 15:13–15)

❤ **children**, **parents** (Ps. 127:3-5
  Exod. 20:12, Eph. 6:1–4)

❤ **home** (Prov. 31:27, Josh. 24:15
  Gal. 6:10, Ps. 127:1)

❤ **church** (Matt. 16:18, Eph. 5:23, Col. 1:24)

❤ **books** (2 Tim. 2:15 KJV)

❤ **creativity** (1 Cor. 10:31)

❤ your **mind**, a healthy **body**
  (Isa. 26:3, Eph. 4:20–24,
  Rom. 12:2, 1 Cor. 6:15)

❤ the **Bible** (Ps. 19:1–11
  Ps. 119:105, Prov. 30:5
  Heb. 4:12)

VERSES OF THE BIBLE THAT ASSURE US OF GOD'S PROTECTION:

Each piece would have the Bible reference stitched or written in fabric paint with a symbol of that promise. Here are some suggestions of symbols and verses to get you started:

❤ the **Red Sea**, parted (Exod. 14:13–23)

❤ **shepherd's rod** and **staff** (Ps. 23:4)

❤ a **city** (Ps. 31:21–24)

❤ a **doorway** (Ps. 121:8)

❤ a **crown** (Ps. 8:5)

❤ an **eagle** (Isa. 40:31)

❤ your **name** (Isa. 43:1)

❤ **God's hand** (Isa. 49:15–16)

❤ **sparrows** (Matt. 10:28–31)

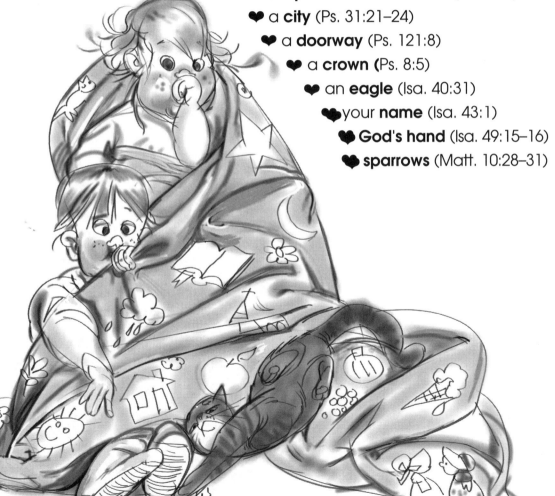

God's "rulers of the night"

Genesis 1:16 says that God created the moon and stars "to rule the night." Since He went to so much trouble to create such an awesome and intricate universe, we should take the time to notice and appreciate what we see in the heavens at night.

♥ Visit a local planetarium to find out which stars and planets are visible in your part of the world.

♥ Schedule a trip to a local observatory where your family can observe the night sky through a powerful telescope.

♥ Learn together the names and placement of the heavenly bodies and how far each is from us in the solar system.

♥ Make a study of the part the sun, moon, and stars play in Bible stories and happenings.

As the young people in your family grow up and move to college, jobs, and homes of their own, they may find themselves in the desert, by the ocean, or in large urban centers or rural communities, some places very different from "home." But God has seen to it that half of what we will all see every day is "sky." If you have learned the sky together as a family, you can always *look up* and find a familiar sight. God's presence and the presence of your family can always be felt as you look at the nighttime sky.

subliminal assurance

Things always seem scarier at night, even for grown-ups.

Choose a tape of some quiet and soothing music that assures you or your child of God's presence while you sleep. Let it play softly as you fall asleep. Here are some kinds of recordings you might like to find:

❤ Instrumental (harp, organ, orchestra) recordings of familiar hymns or gospel songs

❤ Soft classical music

❤ Lullaby recordings especially created to assure young children of God's presence. (See the children's music section in your Christian bookstore or ask the music department manager to suggest something.)

❤ Scripture songs on assurance (Check the listings from Hosanna Praise or Maranatha Music at your local Christian bookstore.)

❤ Recordings of God's creation: the woods, the ocean, the desert, etc. Many recordings combine instrumental hymns or classical music with the sounds of nature.

pillow talk

WHAT'S UNDER THE PILLOW?

There is something very personal about a pillow! Laying your head on a familiar pillow is like settling in with an old friend. It either feels just right, or it doesn't! Kids (and grown-ups) get attached to their own pillows and will fight to keep them.

1 Each night, put an object under your child's pillow. It can be something from nature, like a rock or a leaf, or a favorite object, like a small toy or a picture of a family member.

2 When it is bedtime say, "Let's go see what's under your pillow!" Excitedly hurry to your child's room, climb on the bed, and lift up the pillow to see what's there. Then thank Jesus together for that particular object or the person in the picture. This will help to remind you and your child to be thankful to God for everything in your lives. It is also a lot easier to get excited about going to bed when the child can anticipate a special time of happy surprise with Mom or Dad.

PILLOW TALK CRAFTS

1 Use fabric paints to decorate your own cotton pillowcases with Bible verses and pictures. Fabric paints are washable, and a creative pillowcase also makes a great gift for a friend's birthday or holiday party.

2 When you outgrow a favorite T-shirt, turn it into a pillow. Sew shut the neck, bottom, and one sleeve. Stuff the shirt with polyfill through the remaining sleeve, then sew it closed. Use these pillows on beds or in cozy nooks. If the T-shirt was part of a sports team or church program, the pillow will also remind kids to be thankful for good memories. The shirt will spark conversation when friends visit. (And they're great for pillow fights, too!)

promise pillow

All of us occasionally think of scary or troubling things at night. Sometimes the dark is scary. Before turning out the lights at bedtime, it helps to fill our minds with a promise of God's care and faithfulness while we sleep.

1 Make or buy a small pillow covered with satin or soft flannel. Sew a pocket to one side of the pillow.

2 Write the comforting assurances of God's presence on strips of paper. Choose one to learn for each week. Read it several times each night, then fold it and tuck it into the pocket of your Promise Pillow.

3 By the end of the week you will know the verse from memory. Tape the memorized verse on your bedroom door so you'll see the promises each night as you enter your room.

Choose a new verse at the beginning of each week:

Psalm 127:2	Isaiah 41:10	1 John 5:14–15
Proverbs 3:24	John 14:1	John 14:13–14
Psalm 121:1–2	John 14:27	Philippians 4:8
Psalm 121:3–4	Psalm 23:6	1 Peter 5:6–7
Psalm 121:5–6	1 Peter 3:13	Jeremiah 17:7–8
Psalm 121:7–8	Romans 8:37–39	Psalm 91:10–11
1 Thessalonians 5:8	Philippians 4:13	

teachable moments

A Wise Brother

My five-year-old son is very sharp, so I often ask him to explain the Bible verses we are learning to his little sister in a way a three-year-old can understand. He does extremely well. I recently heard him explaining a psalm to his six-month-old brother. He said, "And when you lay down your little head your slumber will be sweet like you."

—*Rene Ludeman, Colorado Springs, Colorado*

angel watch

Psalm 91:11 says that *"He will command **his angels concerning you** to guard you in all your ways"* (NIV).

Matthew 18:10 tells us that children have angels that watch over them and give account to (and always have the attention of) God Himself. Jesus said, "See that you do not look down on one of these little ones. For I tell you that their angels in heaven always see the face of my Father in heaven."

ANGELS HAVE MANY FUNCTIONS. HERE ARE SOME:

- ❤ They bring messages.
- ❤ They stand guard.
- ❤ They protect.
- ❤ They warn.
- ❤ They make preliminary arrangements or go before us to make a way.
- ❤ They dispel fear.
- ❤ They prevent disaster.

1 Using a different color of poster board or heavy construction paper for each of the functions listed above, cut out angels.

2 Put a small hole in the top of each angel.

3 Use a wire coat hanger to make a mobile to hang over your bed.

4 Use different lengths of thread to attach each angel to the wire mobile so it balances evenly.

5 Look up all the references to angels you can find in the Bible; find a verse for each of the functions. Learn the verse and then write the verse on an angel; specify the function the angel performed in the verse. For example: Luke 2:10—to dispel fear; Exodus 23:20—to prepare the way.

6 Each night before you go to sleep recite one or two of the verses. Go to sleep knowing that God never sleeps and that His angels are at His command concerning you—to guard, protect, warn, inform, and keep you from fear and disaster. Sleep soundly in that assurance.

Teach them to your children . . .
when you rise up.

Deuteronomy 6:7

You probably wouldn't think of going outside without your coat and hat and boots when the snow is blowing, or without a raincoat during a rainstorm. But sometimes we do something even crazier than that: we go into the world—to school or to work—without getting ourselves ready to stand strong against the attacks of Satan or the influences of the world around us.

When our minds are rested and alert is a very important time to hide the Word in our hearts. The Bible talks about putting on the equipment of a good soldier: the breastplate of righteousness, the helmet of salvation, the shoes of preparation of the gospel of peace, the shield of faith, and the sword of the Spirit, which is the Word of God.

Before your family goes out into the weather today, make sure they are protected with the Word of God. Here are some ways to do just that!

Section 10

hanging your prayers out to dry

Spring is the rainy season. The storm clouds roll across the sky and bump into each other with bursts of thunder. Some noisy spring rains are frightening, but the puddles they leave behind are fun to splash in when the sun comes out. There is a fresh smell as the sun's warm rays dry the clouds' tears and leave the landscape a clean, bright green.

Families experience cloudy times in their lives too. Sometimes we feel sad, and our tearful words can sound like angry thunder. We all need patience to watch for the sunshine. Some lessons about prayer can only be learned during these turbulent seasons. Just as the weather is in God's hands, families can understand their needs are in God's hands.

1 Cut storm clouds out of gray construction paper.

2 Cut out smiling yellow sun faces just a little larger than the clouds.

MAKE A PRAYER CLOTHESLINE

3 Hang a clothesline rope in the family room, bedroom, or entryway. (Make sure it's out of the way so no one runs into it.)

4 Write prayer requests on the gray clouds.

5 Remember your requests as you pray each morning before you leave for work or school and as you discuss the storms of life.

6 Write God's promises for each need on the clouds.

WHEN GOD ANSWERS PRAYER

1 When a prayer is answered, hang a bright yellow sun on the clothesline over the gray cloud.

2 Write a praise verse on the sun.

3 Rejoice in God's presence in the tough times and His provisions on dark days. Soon the clothesline will have sunshine among the rain clouds—just like in real life!

160

bear one another's burdens

1 Share a secret prayer project with one person in the family by praying together for some special need or situation that is troubling another family member (like money to go to college, direction for a new vocational opportunity, confirmation about marriage plans, being accepted into an educational program, etc.). You may want to reveal to other family members your commitment to pray together when the prayer has been answered.

2 Make a pact with your whole family to pray consistently about something affecting the family (like a possible move, a financial crisis, a friend your family hopes to lead to God) or a problem or need outside the family (a new pastor for your church, a change in a school policy, a situation in your community, a national leader).

3 Keep a family journal of answered prayer.

protection against the elements

Just as you need warm clothes to protect you from winter's cold, you also need to be sure your spiritual well-being is warmly "dressed" in the protection of God's Word. So that you will remember how important it is to read God's Word before leaving for your day, mark your winter clothing with verses from the reference in Ephesians.

1 BOOTS—Use a piece of colored tape inside or on the sole of your boot. Write in black permanent marker: "My feet are shod with the preparation of the gospel" (Eph. 6:15 NKJV)

2 Sew labels inside each article of clothing on which you have written with permanent ink:

COAT—Breastplate of righteousness (Eph. 6:14)

 SCARF—The belt of truth (Eph. 6:14)

 HAT—The helmet of salvation (Eph. 6:17)

3 Pray together before each person in your family leaves for work or school so that you may be equipped with:

♥ The shield of faith (Eph. 6:16), which can extinguish all the flaming darts of the enemy

♥ The sword of the spirit, which is the Word of God (Eph. 6:17)

♥ Prayer (Eph. 6:18)

MAKE "BLESSING" A PART OF YOUR DAY AND A THEME OF YOUR LIFE. HERE ARE SOME WAYS:

the blessing

The idea of "blessing" is a strong principle throughout the Bible. Children need their parents' blessing, soldiers going to battle need the blessing of their superiors, we need the blessing of each other, and we all need God's blessing on our lives. There are even Scripture verses that tell us we can "bless God" by the way we obey and praise Him.

♥ Pray God's blessing on the day before you even get out of bed.

♥ Bless the food and each other as you gather around the breakfast table.

♥ Husbands, bless your wives by affirming them and assuring them of your love, faithfulness, and esteem for what they are doing.

♥ Wives, bless your husbands by telling them you love them, trust them, and will be praying for them all day.

♥ Children, bless your parents by telling them you are proud of them and promise to represent your home with honor and integrity.

♥ Parents, give your children your blessing before they leave for school, and pray together asking God to use them as a witness to His and your family's love for others they meet.

❁ Bless the "mission" or the special assignment you've been given for this day such as:

➺ a business trip assigned by your boss or company

➺ presiding over an important meeting

➺ contact with someone who is hurting

➺ being a caregiver for someone who is discouraged, ill, or has a new baby

➺ representing your class or team at a special scholastic event

➺ taking an entrance exam for promotion or college

➺ gathering neighborhood friends for a Bible study

➺ beginning a new grade, new school location, new school opportunity, new job

♥ Write your blessing and stick it on the dashboard of the car, mail it in a letter to a family member in college or military service, or leave it on someone's pillow if you're going to be away for a while.

♥ Look up "bless" or "blessing" in a good Bible concordance and spend family worship time reading together about the times the principles of blessing are used in God's Word.

SUGGESTION: A good book on the importance of blessing is *The Gift of the Blessing* by Gary Smalley and John Trent (Thomas Nelson, 1993).

The Surprise Blessing

The time had come. Paying tuition for three children in Christian schools was becoming an impossibility. Soon our fourth child would enter kindergarten. We had to do what all of us dreaded . . . we enrolled in the public school system. This was the first day of school. My precious first-grader and I bravely drove the two blocks it took to get there.

As we pulled into the parking lot I looked at Jenny. Having spent one year in the safe environment of a loving Christian kindergarten, she was convinced she was entering the land of the heathen. Genuine fear was written on her face. How could I help her face this difficult situation? Nothing I said made her smile. Finally, I did what seemed to be silly, but what God was saying to do. I blessed her. Placing my hand on her head, I prayed, "The LORD bless you and keep you; the LORD make His (smiling) face shine upon you . . . and give you peace." (See Numbers 6:24–26.)

After she left, I stayed in the car, praying for her and for the school, and thinking about

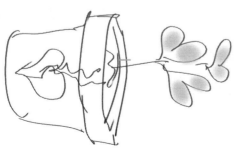

blessing Jenny. I could not remember being blessed by my parents when I was a child. Where did this idea come from? I had never blessed my children before, never put my hand on their heads and pronounced God's blessing on them. Just doing it made me realize that the Bible is full of examples of people blessing their children. Joseph, Jacob, Isaac . . . to name a few, put great store in the words they prayed over a child's head. What a powerful tool God had put in my hands!

As the years went by and the fourth child, Crystal, went to school, this blessing became a habit. Because her dad took her sometimes, she taught him to do it. If I forgot, she reminded me. This time with her was a daily joy to me.

The time with Jenny, however, had become difficult. She was in junior high, the age when no one wanted to be different. She still wanted to be blessed, but her plea was, "Mom, please, don't let any of my friends see us!" I found it hard not to laugh since the prayer was very short and done in a car with the windows rolled up. "Okay, Jen, I'll make it short, and I won't put my hand on your head." So I put my hand on her shoulder, but in my heart it always rested on her head.

One day Jenny shyly came into my room and put a note on my desk. In it she thanked me for praying for her. Included in the note was a little card for my wallet imprinted with "our" blessing. It was her way of returning the blessing to me. A simple act on her part—a sweet message from God: *This is something I have established.* I know it will carry on into our adult lives together and it will sound even sweeter as "Grandma's blessing."

—*Kathy Maxwell, Monrovia, California*

family signals

After Jesus went back to his Father, His disciples had some rough times. It was dangerous for them to even talk about Jesus to each other in public sometimes and they had to worship Him together in secret meeting places. Often when they met they would draw the sign of the fish in the sand on the beach or in the dust of the road. This was like a greeting of encouragement to keep strong in their faith.

Invent signals that only your family knows, and encourage each other with your secret sign. Here are some suggestions:

♥ Wink, tug on an earlobe, touch your nose, or give an "Okay" sign with your fingers in a crowded room or from a distance (like on the football or soccer field, basketball floor, tennis court, during an audition, or across the church).

♥ Draw a smiley face or other happy character on notes, or paint them on fingernails, homework papers, or napkins in lunchboxes.

♥ Whenever the early church gathered, someone would confirm the gift of new life in Christ by saying, "Christ is risen!" Then everyone would affirm that truth with the enthusiastic response: "He is risen, indeed!" Try using this greeting and response with your family and Christian friends.

♥ Invent a funny or unusual word or phrase that has meaning only to your family to be whispered in passing, written on notes, or spoken on the phone.

you can always reach God... and me

"Now unto him that is able to keep you from falling, and to present you faultless before the presence of his glory with exceeding joy, to the only wise God our Savior, be glory and majesty, dominion and power, both now and ever. Amen"
Jude 1:24-25 (KJV).

♥ Make a habit of letting others in the family know where you are and where you can be reached by leaving plans, itineraries, and phone numbers when you have to be out of town or simply by leaving notes on the kitchen counter or bathroom mirror when you're going out.

♥ Help each other remember that God is always "just a prayer away" by leaving Scripture references as you would phone numbers with the reminder: "You can reach Him anytime." Here are some examples:

"EVENING, AND MORNING, AND AT NOON, I WILL PRAY, AND CRY ALOUD, AND HE SHALL HEAR MY VOICE"
(PS. 55:17 NKJV).

"I thank my God every time I remember you, always praying with joy." for all of you"
(Phil. 1:3-4).

"Keep yourselves in the love of God, looking for the mercy of our Lord Jesus Christ unto eternal life"
(Jude 1:21 NKJV).

"God began doing a good work in you, and I am sure He will continue it until it is finished when Jesus Christ comes again"
(Phil. 1:6).

breakfast peace

Most families are made up of very different personalities. Some may be "morning people"; some may be "night owls." Scurrying to get ready for the day can cause chaos. To prevent arguing or getting on each other's nerves at the breakfast table, use this time to read a story from a good Bible storybook. Choose one that appeals to the ages of your children. (Suggestions of great Bible storybooks for all ages can be found in the Resources section.) This will help the family share both physical and spiritual food and nourish each person for the day. It will also make breakfast a lot more pleasant.

teachable moments

School Prayer

Dear Lord,

Please hold his little hand
When I cannot be there;
Surround him with Your angels,
And keep him in Your care.

Bring to his mind the wisdom
We've shared throughout the years,
And hold him with Your comfort
To banish all his fears.

Lord, help me to believe You'll
Care for him like me;
And teach him when I'm gone
It's Your face he can see.

—Written by Marybeth Cuccie of Venice,
Florida, for her son, Christopher Russell Cuccie.

Remember these commands . . .
write them down.

Deuteronomy 6:8

*A*re you a list maker? It's hard to remember life before "sticky

pads"! In our families we all need reminders, so at our

houses we stick notes everywhere: on the counter by the sink, on

the refrigerator, on the bathroom mirror, on the

headboard of the bed, on the steering wheel of the car . . .

everywhere! We write dozens of reminders—so we won't forget.

Writing them down is a good way to remember the most important things,

including the commandments and the promises of God. There's

just something about the very act of writing things down that helps us

to remember (even when we forget to take our lists with us)!

Here are some ways to write down life's most important reminders.

writing the Word

Section 11

a name is a gift

There are times when we don't like our names or we want to experiment with other more exciting or glamorous names. Sometimes friends give us nicknames whether or not we like it. Names are very importantand often have special meaning.

Each person's name has a special meaning, history, or significance. Discuss as a family each person's name. Here are some questions to answer:

♥ What does your name mean? (There are many good books that tell the meanings of names at your library or bookstore.)

♥ Why was your particular name chosen?

♥ Were you named after someone special?

♥ What hopes for your life does your name convey?

♥ What do you feel when you hear your name?

♥ Choose a special Bible verse that would go with your name.

♥ Look up the origin and heritage of your name. (You may want to research family records or talk to grandparents or other older relatives.)

♥ A name can be a gift to help shape a child's identity. How do you think you've been "shaped" by your name?

♥ Make a study of the name of each person in your extended family.

♥ Why did God sometimes change people's names? If God changed your name because of something you've learned or some new talent you've developed, what might you be called?

"A good name is more desirable than great riches" (Prov. 22:1 NIV).

There are often opportunities in your family to help choose a good name: for dolls, stuffed animals, pets, and new babies in the family. These times can lead to great discussions and even a little research on the meaning of names. A good Bible dictionary will assist in the search.

choosing a good name

Here are some Bible questions to get your family started thinking about names:

💜 Why did Rebekah name her son Esau? (See Genesis 25:21–26).

💜 Why was Sarah's son named Isaac? (See Genesis 17:17–19; 18:9–15; 21:3–6).

💜 What does Obadiah's name tell us about him? (See Bible dictionary).

💜 Why was Gideon called Jerub-Baal? (See Judges 6:28–32).

💜 Who told Mary to call her son Jesus? (See Luke 1:26–33).

💜 New pets are a big responsibility for the whole family. Naming the pet is very important. Work together to choose a name that reflects the personality and special abilities of your pet.

💜 New brothers and sisters are exciting. When a new baby is on the way, have everyone in the family bring a list of names that he or she likes. Research the names to see what they mean. Imagine the name on a grown-up. Will it still "fit" when the baby isn't little anymore? Will you allow nicknames? If not, agree together to encourage people outside the family to call the baby by its real name. Make a sign for the baby's room or buy lettered blocks to spell out the baby's name on a dressertop or shelf.

💜 Dolls and stuffed animals seem to have their own personalities. Sometimes they even come with their own pretend birth certificates. Use your imagination to come up with names that reflect the personality of particular play-friends. Make nametags so you can see how a name is spelled and how the letters sound.

God-is-faithful journal

Buy a blank book or journal at a bookstore and keep it in your book bag or car glove compartment. Whenever you think of a Bible verse you've learned or read that relates to something in your day, write down the incident and the verse.

Whenever you see an answer to prayer or an example of the truth of Scripture (a promise, a warning, a story of human nature or God's grace) write it down and also write the corresponding Bible truth.

Over the months and years you will begin to see how very important God's Word is to instruct, warn, encourage, direct, and comfort you. It *really* works in the "dailyness" of our lives.

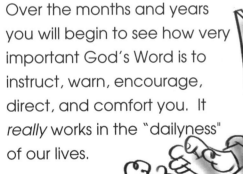

bible notes from home

Before your child leaves for camp, college, military service, or for a semester abroad, write notes of encouragement on sticky notes and attach them to pages of your child's Bible where special texts of hope, instruction, or promise are found. As your child has his or her daily devotions, he or she will come across assurances of both your love and support and the steadfast love of the heavenly Father.

Children can also write notes to their parents. Put encouraging notes in your mother or father's day-planner or calendar. Leave notes in their Bible before they leave on a trip. Put Bible verses of blessings in suitcases, makeup bags, or shaving kits.

telephone promise reminder

"Call to me and I will answer you and tell you great and unsearchable things you do not know" (Jer. 33:3 NIV).

1 Copy this verse on a sticky pad. Stick it on your telephone and leave it there until the whole family can quote this verse.

2 Make a pact with a friend that every time you call each other on the telephone you will say, "Hello," . . . then quote this verse.

3 Make a decorative cover for the phone books in your house using this verse.

4 In your family address book write the reference of a Bible promise under some or all of the phone numbers. Each time you reach for the book to call your friends, you will be reminded to claim a promise for them, too.

PRAYER LINE
Some churches and organizations have a prayer chain or prayer hotline. If your church operates one of these services, keep its phone number posted by your telephone. This is a good way to call upon the Lord through the prayers of God's faithful people.

who wrote it?

A letter is a very personal form of communication. We all like to get mail from friends and relatives. The New Testament contains many letters; the authors of the books of the Bible wrote very personal messages to us. To make this fact a little more real, do this exercise with biblical texts your family is learning.

1 Try to discover: Who wrote this Bible message? To whom was it originally written?

2 Discuss what the message might mean to your family.

3 Write the Bible text in letter form. (Some of the books are already written this way. They're called *epistles*.)

4 Mail them weekly to each other.

5 Write Bible letters to friends or answer the letters in the Bible by responding to the Bible authors.

SAMPLE BIBLE LETTER
(See Ephesians 1:15–19a, 6:23 NIV.)
You can also find letters in the Old Testament.

Dear *Molly*

Ever since I heard about your faith in the Lord Jesus and your love for all the saints, I have not stopped giving thanks for you, remembering you in my prayers.

I pray also that the eyes of your heart may be enlightened in order that you may know the hope to which he has called you, the riches of his incomparable great power for us who believe.

I keep asking that the God of our Lord Jesus Christ, the glorious Father, may give you the Spirit of wisdom and revelation, so that you may know Him better.

Peace to the whole family,

Paul

creating bible rhymes

Nursery rhymes are favorites with children young and old. These simple verses encourage good listening and help develop language skills. Jackie Nolen of Concord, California, says her children enjoy creating Bible rhymes.

ONE OF HER FAVORITES IS:

David was a shepherd boy.

David was a king.

David liked to play the harp.

David liked to sing!

1 Use Sunday school lessons or Bible storybooks to help your family learn about a Bible character.

2 Use a dictionary or thesaurus to look up rhyming words.

3 Work together to create a rhyme, or let family members work individually or in pairs, then see who comes up with the most creative verse.

4 Encourage the whole family to memorize the rhyme.

5 Collect the Bible rhymes in a scrapbook.

6 Complete the scrapbook with art illustrations.

lunch notes

When you pack a lunch for someone else in the family, send encouraging messages with Scripture verses chosen to relate to their day.

Put a smiley-face sticker on one item in the lunchbag or box (on the sandwich wrapper, cupcake wrapper, granola-bar wrapper, apple peel, etc). Change the location each day so that searching for the sticker becomes a daily adventure.

"BEHOLD, THE EYE OF THE LORD IS ON THOSE WHO FEAR HIM, ON THOSE WHO HOPE FOR HIS LOVINGKINDNESS."
PSALM 33:18
(NAS)

THE LORD WATCH BETWEEN ME AND THEE WHILE

Create a special cartoon character that always bears an encouraging (or humorous, or instructional) message, and draw it on the napkins.

Put in the lunchbag or box a Scripture card from the treasure boxes of Bible verses you can buy at Christian bookstores, or make your own on 3 x 5 cards.

With a fine-point pen encircle a hard-boiled egg with a special promise for the day. For instance, write out Genesis 31:49.

teachable moments

Pictures in the Dirt

As a preschool child I often visited my grandparents on their farm. Those were always exciting times. My grandfather loved to tell me great stories from the Bible. He would often stop, stoop down, and draw pictures for me in the dirt.

They were simple pictures, of course, but today as an adult, I remember every detail of those stories as though I heard them yesterday. How I praise God for a faithful, godly grandfather!

—*Barbara Neal, Columbus, Ohio*

grace notes

Everyone needs encouragement, forgiveness, and reminders of God's (and each other's) love. Notes left around the house are a good way to help each other make it through hard days and keep you going on good days.

Use brightly colored sticky-pads to write special notes to your family. Sometimes just a word from the Word is best.

Stick notes in places like:

♥ bathroom mirror

♥ school bag

♥ dashboard of car

♥ bed pillow

♥ bed headboard

♥ kitchen cabinet door

♥ suitcase

♥ school assignment book

♥ lunchbox

♥ refrigerator door

teachable moments

A Name Is an Anchor

Roberta Lynn Strickler of Arcanum, Ohio, is proud of her middle name. Her mother came to know Christ in Lynn, Indiana, and that is why she chose Lynn as Roberta's middle name. When Roberta's mother sang to her, she often inserted her name into songs about God's love and protection. These memories have always drawn Roberta back to Christ and given her a sense of security.

"A good name is more desirable than great riches." (*Prov. 22:1 NIV*).

Tie them on your forehead
to remind you.

Deuteronomy 6:8

Could the Scripture really be written on our foreheads? Well, perhaps it could.

But there are lots of other ways to wear reminders on our bodies

so we won't forget. Rings, headbands, bracelets, T-shirts and sweatshirts,

belts, and necklaces can all remind us to keep the commandments

of the Lord. So could bumper stickers, banners, decals, and sidewalk art.

All of these ideas could help us to write God's Word, not only on our

foreheads but also on our brains and in our hearts.

This could be fun!

Section

12

the secret fish

MAKE A SECRET FISH SYMBOL

"Every day they continued to meet together . . . They broke bread in their homes . . . praising God"
(Acts 2: 46–47 NIV).

1 Collect some styrofoam meat-packing trays.

2 Punch holes in the trays with an ice pick in the shape of a a fish.

3 Use colored yarn and a blunt plastic needle to sew the picture. Make a yarn hanger on top.

SECRET MEETINGS

In the years that followed Jesus' death and resurrection, the early Christians suffered a lot of persecution from wicked rulers. They often had to meet in secret to worship together. They changed their secret meeting place each time and used the symbol of a fish to mark the spot where they met. The outline of a fish could be drawn and erased quickly before Roman guards found it. The fish stood for life and happiness.

4 Hang the fish in the "secret" place where your family will meet today for prayer. See if other family members can find it.

I	-	JESUS
X	-	CHRIST
O	-	GOD'S
Y	-	SON
C	-	SAVIOR

Look up the word *fish* in a Bible dictionary. The Greek word for fish is *IXOYC*. The letters stand for the Greek words meaning "Jesus Christ, God's Son Savior."

Kids can draw the fish or the Greek word IXOYC on their school notebooks to identify with other Christians in school.

a prayer necklace

"Pray continually, and give thanks whatever happens"
(1 Thess. 5:17).

How do you pray? Do you kneel? Do you lie in your bed? Do you fold your hands and close your eyes? There is no right way or wrong way to pray. God welcomes us to talk to Him anytime, and He is comfortable with us in any position. We should always be reverent in our prayers—that means to show honor and respect to God.

The German monks of the fourteenth and fifteenth centuries always bowed and covered their heads with the hood of their robes. The monks folded their arms across their chest to make an X, which is a form of the cross of Christ. Since they prayed all day and did not leave their home (called a monastery), they needed to find a way to support themselves financially. So they baked and sold little breads called brezel, or pretzel. The cross shape of the pretzel reminded people to pray continually.

MAKE HOMEMADE PRETZELS

💜 Use ribbon or yarn to string the pretzels into a necklace.

💜 Each pretzel can represent a special praise or prayer request.

💜 Kids can wear the necklace to school to remind them to pray during the day.

💜 Share the necklace as an after-school snack so you can discuss the importance of prayer with friends.

Recipe for homemade pretzels:
* 1 1/2 cups warm water
* 1 packet yeast
* 1 tsp. salt
* 1 tsp. sugar
* 4 cups flour
* 1 egg
* coarse salt

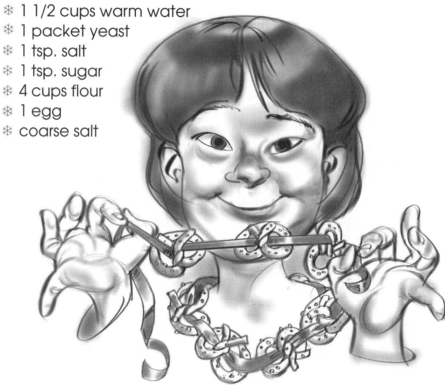

Dissolve the yeast in warm water. Next add salt and sugar. Blend in flour. Knead dough until smooth. Cut into small pieces. Roll in ropes and twist into shape. Place on lightly greased cookie sheets. Brush the pretzels with a beaten egg. Finally, sprinkle with coarse salt. Bake at 425 degrees for 12–15 minutes.

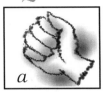
a

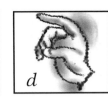
b

c

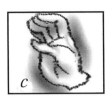
d

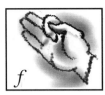
e

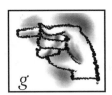
f

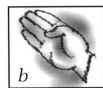
g

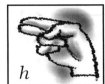
h

z

silent truths

"Be still, and know that I am God" (Ps. 46:10 KJV).

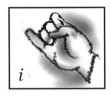
i

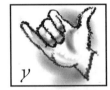
y

Did you know there is a language you cannot hear?
It is not spoken with the lips.
It is spoken with hands.
It is a special, beautiful language.
It is called *sign language.*

Sign language is a visual way of making Scripture "come alive" and helping your family better understand and communicate with those who cannot hear.

In some churches there is a seating section for those who are hearing impaired. In front of this section, a person who has studied sign language will sign during the service. During the song service they will all sign a song together. It is beautiful to watch. It can also be observed on television in some areas. Check your local program guides.

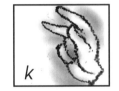
J

x

j

k

💜 Photocopy these signs and put them in a notebook.

💜 Practice "saying" the names of each family member in sign language.

l

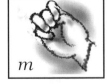
w

💜 Share a "silent truth" from God's Word with your family before your evening meal or at bedtime.

💜 Add Bible verses to your book in sign language.

Recommended reading:
Sign Language for Everyone by Cathy Rice (Thomas Nelson, 1977).

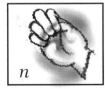
m

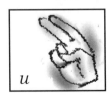
v

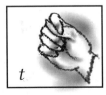
u

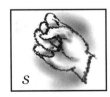
t

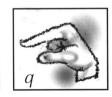
s

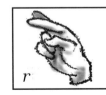
r

q

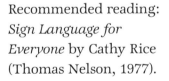
p

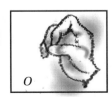
o

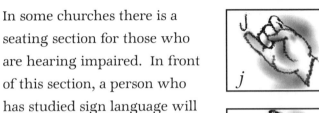
n

armbands

Sometimes armbands are worn to show that someone belongs to a particular branch of the military or to organizations like Boy Scouts or Campfire Girls.

Make armbands to show that you belong to the army of the Lord.

1 Cut strips of construction paper or lightweight poster board slightly longer than the circumference of your arm. Glue or staple ends together, overlapping edges.

> Note: For longer-lasting armbands, use stretchy knit cloth, cutting the strips a bit shorter so that they will stretch to stay snug on arm.

2 Cut out symbols or phrases from felt or contact paper and stick-glue or sew to armbands.

Here are some other ideas for designs, but yours will probably be even better!

Bible reference t-shirt

As you memorize Bible passages, keep a record of the verses on a 5 x 7 card taped to the refrigerator. When the card is full, paint the references in many bright colors on a white or colored T-shirt. Special fabric paints are available in craft stores or the craft section of discount stores. Follow instructions for the type of paint selected.

As you wear your shirt, practice reciting the verses by looking at the references.

what do they say behind my back?

1 Write the names of several Bible characters on pieces of paper and pin them to each person's back. Do not let the person see the name he or she is wearing.

2 When the game begins, everyone moves around the room asking others, "What do they say behind my back?" The other person then answers with a detail about the Bible character's life, habits, disposition, or behavior, beginning each response with "Well, they say you . . .." Try to choose lesser-known facts so the person doesn't guess his or her biblical identity right away.

3 As soon as the person guesses correctly, he or she can sit down, but each tries to keep the others from guessing and sitting down before he or she does.

4 The one who stays standing the longest is the loser.

"think" headbands

5 Hide the message in the secret pocket of your headband. When you are alone, take it out and read it. Try to memorize it by the end of the week.

1 At a discount or variety store buy an inexpensive stretchy headband at least one inch wide.

2 Cut a piece of cloth two inches long and slightly narrower than the headband.

4 Each week type a secret message to yourself on a strip of paper. Choose one of the many verses from God's Word that tells us how we should or shouldn't *think.*

6 After you learn your "thinkverse" put it on a bulletin board in your room. You might want to make a big cutout of your head from poster board and glue the strips to it as you learn the verses.

3 Sew the strip of cloth carefully to the inside of the headband, attaching both ends and one side to make a secret pocket.

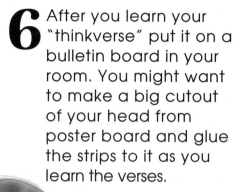

Choose a new "think verse" for each new week. Here are some suggestions for you:

- 💜 Proverbs 23:7
- 💜 Isaiah 2:5
- 💜 Matthew 5:17–18
- 💜 Mark 12:30
- 💜 Luke 12:29–31
- 💜 Acts 13:25 and 17:29
- 💜 Romans 2:1–3 and 12:2, 3,16
- 💜 1 Corinthians 13:5
- 💜 2 Corinthians 10:2
- 💜 Galatians 6:3
- 💜 Ephesians 3:20
- 💜 Philippians 2:5 and 4:2, 8

THE LORD IS NEAR

bible t-shirt painting party

1 Invite friends to a shirt-painting party. Have everyone bring a plain cotton T-shirt. (Craft stores and T-shirt outlets have the best prices.) You will need to supply:

- ♥ Fabric paints in various colors
- ♥ Large pieces of cardboard (Pieces cut in the shape of a T-shirt are available at craft stores.)
- ♥ A big piece of plastic or newspaper to cover the workspace
- ♥ Pencils and paper

2 Insert the cardboard inside the shirt to keep the paint from leaking through to the back of the shirt and to make a firm drawing surface.

3 First, have each person draw a design related to his or her favorite Bible verse. Simple illustrations or decorations may be used as well as the words.

4 Pull the shirt tightly around the cardboard and draw the basic design on the cloth with a pencil.

5 Paint the design onto the shirt.

6 When your design is finished, let the shirts dry on a table or hang them on a clothesline. Serve refreshments and play games or make sidewalk drawings while the shirts are drying.

7 Have everyone take the shirts home, but be careful not to touch the paint for twenty-four hours.

driveway art contest

1 Invite friends (both kids and adults) to choose their favorite Bible story or verse and illustrate it by drawing with sidewalk chalk on your driveway.

2 Try to guess what the story is by looking at the drawing.

3 Give prizes for the best drawing and the most subtle illustration (the one hardest to guess).

4 After all the stories have been guessed, write the Bible reference below each drawing.

5 Serve chips and soda or lemonade or have a picnic.

Bible costume race

1 Form two lines of equal numbers of boys and girls. (Parents can play too!)

2 Across the floor from the front of each line, place a box that contains a Bible costume. The box across from the girls' line should contain a woman's costume; the box across from the boys' line should have a man's costume.

3 When the leader blows a trumpet, (or says "go") the first person in each line races to the box, puts on the costume, runs back to tag the next person in line, races back to the box, takes off the costume and returns it to the box, and goes to the end of the line. Person #2 then runs to the box, puts on the costume, etc., until everyone in line has worn the costume and returned to the line. The first team to finish wins.

Some costume ideas might be:

♥ an "Esther the Queen" costume with purple satin robe, sparkled crown, gold rope or sash, sandals with glitter, and a scepter.

♥ a "Virgin Mary" costume with a blue cotton garment, white head scarf, blue headband to hold the scarf, dark blue sash, and simple shoes.

♥ a "Moses" costume with heavy robe, lace-up sandals, a beard, a sash, long vest, a rod, and a tablet of "stone."

♥ a "Goliath" costume with breastplate, helmet, leg guards, and sword.

Write them
on your doors and gates.

Deuteronomy 6:9

*T*he entry and exit places of our lives should have God's mark all over them.

This means not only the real doors and gates of our houses and

driveways, but also the entrances and exits of our lifetimes—the passages

we go through on our way to maturity.

Perhaps one of the reasons it is becoming so hard for kids to grow up

and take responsibility is that we have lost many of our

rituals or rites of passage. Here are some ways we can put the mark

of God's Word on the gateways of our lives and celebrate what

we are becoming as His children.

HIDING THE WORD

in the passages of our lives

Section 13

The celebration of Pentecost is described in both the Old and New Testaments. The word *Pentecost* means "fifty."

In the Old Testament the Jewish feast day came fifty days after the Passover Feast. It began the summer harvest of wheat; on our calendar today it falls in mid-May. Look at Leviticus 23, where another name for this day is the Feast of the Weeks.

In the New Testament the Day of Pentecost took place fifty days after the resurrection of Jesus. It was the day God kept His promise to give the Holy Spirit to Jesus' disciples. Read the story in Acts 2:1–12. The Day of Pentecost is also called the birthday of the New Testament church.

3 Tape symbols for the following objects to the ends of the yarn and hang the mobile over the kitchen table the week before Pentecost Sunday.

- ♥ wheat of the harvest (Lev. 23:16)
- ♥ cloud or wind (Acts 2:2)
- ♥ flames of fire (Acts 2:3)
- ♥ dove of the Holy Spirit (Matt. 3:16)
- ♥ tongues of native languages (Acts 2:5–12)
- ♥ the apostle Peter, who preached that day (Acts 2:14)

the day of pentecost

SIGNS-OF-PENTECOST MOBILE

To celebrate Pentecost, make a mobile with symbols representing the events of this special day.

1 Cut a strip of colored paper 2 inches wide by 18 inches long and tape it to form a circle. The circle represents the "circle of believers" who met in the Upper Room.

2 Cut 6 pieces of yarn 26 inches long and tie them together at one end to form the top of the mobile. Tape yarn at equal distant points on the inside of the circle, letting the ends hang down to hold the symbols.

4 After Pentecost week hang your mobile in an entrance or exit (hallway, entryway, archway to the living room) so that in your family's comings and goings the symbols will be a reminder of the ongoing presence of the Holy Spirit.

postcard posters

About the time kids stop bringing home cute little pictures to hang on the refrigerator, they start sticking pictures from teen magazines and assorted posters on their bedroom walls.

Posters are a great way to keep Bible truths before your children's eyes.

1 Look for bright, exciting action postcards or wall posters such as crashing ocean waves, snowy ski slopes, mountain climbers, etc.

2 Type a Bible verse that relates to the picture; for example, with a photo of rock climbers, write:

💜 *"When you are tempted, he will also provide a way out so that you can stand up under it" (1 Cor. 10:13 NIV).*

💜 *When you feel like you can't hang on any longer . . . look for God's hand to lift you up!*

3 Paste the picture and the typed message on a colorful piece of construction paper. Stationery with colorful borders can also work well.

Use a frame or laminate the poster for hanging.
Hang it in your teenager's bathroom, beside the game table in the rec room, or on the ceiling above his or her bed!

Note : You may want to simply afix strips of colored paper with scripture messages to large posters found in travel and frame shops.

193

celebrate the coming of age

The passage into adulthood is an important one and should be celebrated with the community of important adults of the same gender in a young person's life. Plan a gathering of women (for girls) or men (for boys) by inviting friends to a "coming-of-age celebration."

This may be done when the young person enters high school, when he or she passes the sixteenth birthday, or when he or she graduates from high school, depending on the family's wishes.

Send invitations asking significant adults to bring a letter to the young person telling what his or her life has meant to the adult, what they wish for him or her, and what text of Scripture has been meaningful for that adult as he or she has gone through the various experiences of life.

The celebration may be a formal, dress-up affair with a special meaning and time of sharing, or it may be as informal as a cookout or pizza party. The important thing is for the same-gender parent to make a significant statement about the value of this child and the importance of ushering him or her into this grown-up part of the journey. It is also important for the child to feel the support and exaltations of the adults in his or her life.

HERE ARE SOME IDEAS FOR THIS CELEBRATION:

❤ A campout with the sharing time around a campfire

❤ A private brunch at a restaurant or home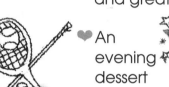

❤ A golf or tennis tournament followed by a lunch, dinner, or refreshments

❤ A barbeque with western clothing and decorations

❤ A driver's-license party with road signs, maps, and driving instructions for the road of life

❤ An overnight fishing or hunting trip together

❤ A book party— Guests bring great books on topics like leadership, goal setting, decisions, and great literature.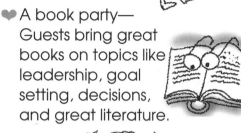

❤ An evening dessert party

❤ A formal garden party

❤ A vocational party with gifts and decorations geared toward the child's special interest or ability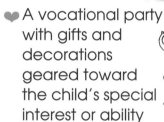

❤ A linen party for the young person's future (guests bring bed linens, towels, etc.)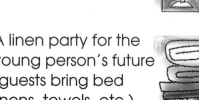

a garden of my own

Mark a child's entrance into the "age of responsibility" (ages five through seven) by giving him or her a garden plot to design, plant, and care for. The space may be as small as three feet by four feet, but give the child ownership of it. You will need to till the space for the child and mix in fertilizer, compost and (if soil is very dense like clay) builder's sand. Then help the child choose seed and show him or her how to make straight rows by pounding stakes at each end and stretching string between the stakes.

❤ Let the child choose both flowers and vegetables. These can be separated by color and height, or mixed together.

❤ Help the child water and watch for sprouts to come up. Teach him or her the difference between weeds and blades of grass (which must be pulled) and the seedlings he or she has planted.

❤ Make a special meal of the first vegetables from the child's garden.

❤ Talk about how much work goes into the food we enjoy every day.

Many Bible verses and stories have to do with seeds, plants, growing, harvesting, and cultivating. Help your child locate as many as he or she can find by looking up the words listed below in a good Bible dictionary or concordance. Encourage him or her to learn as many verses as possible before the crop is ready to be harvested.

Garden Scriptures:
- sower
- seed
- harvest
- farmer
- plants

STAKES FOR
CLIMBING BEAN PLANTS

ROWS OF SEEDS

CIRCLE OF FLOWERS

a scripture shadowbox

Starting a collection is a good hobby. Collections also help us remember the "passages" in our life; they are a sort of journal of our life's history. Some popular collections feature stamps, rocks, shells, and coins. These collections can teach us about history, geography, art, and science.

Did you ever think of Scripture verses as a personal collection? Do you enjoy water sports? Then you will like Bible stories that take place on the beach or at sea. Do you like to plant gardens? Then you will want to look up all the flowers in the Bible to discover why and how they were used in Scripture. There are many topics of verses you could choose: animals, miracles, objects, tools, weapons, and symbols. Here's how to get started:

1 Choose a topic for your family's collection of Bible verses.

2 Buy or build a shadowbox with ten to twelve small sections to hang on the wall.

3 Use a Bible concordance or dictionary to make a list of verses that refer to your collection.

4 Read one story and/or memorize one verse each week.

5 Collect small objects to represent each Bible reference.

6 Watch your collection grow as you enjoy learning.

7 Pass out the objects as your family reviews the stories or verses.

8 Share your collection with friends who visit your home.

9 Discover what each object tells us about God and about ourselves.

For example, here is a collection of Bible references to animals (all verses are KJV except where noted):

- ♥ Lions:
  Judges 14:5-6
  1 Samuel 17:34-37
  Psalm 104:21
  Proverbs 30:30
  Revelation 5:5

- ♥ Gazelle (roe, or hart):
  Deuteronomy 12:15, 22
  2 Samuel 2:18
  Proverbs 6:5

- ♥ Rock badger:
  Psalm 104:18
  Proverbs 30:26 (NCV)

- ♥ Sheep:
  1 Samuel 17:34
  Luke 15:1–7

- ♥ Foxes:
  Judges 15:4

- ♥ Horse:
  Exodus 14:9, 23
  Joshua 11:4
  1 Kings 10:26–29
  Esther 6:8–11

when things are tough

Bad things happen in life. When someone in your family is going through hard times, here are some things you can do to help along with related resources from God's Word.

- Be sensitive enough to notice that there is a problem.
- Never belittle each other's feelings. (Don't ever say, "Big boys don't cry.")
- Learn to know each other so well that you can "read" each other, even when you're not talking.
- Get him or her to talk about the problem, then really listen with your heart.
- Give him or her top priority when crises arise in his or her life.
- Don't wait for it to pass. It may, but he or she may bury resentments in the process.
- Be honest about discussing the situation. Parents don't have to be God; they aren't perfect. They are just parents. Children are smart and sensitive to your deeper feelings; don't lie to them. Admit failures, lack of abilities, shortcomings of your own (to the point that their emotions can cope with it). Sometimes admitting your own faults (the kids already know you have them) will help them face theirs.
- Forgive the source of the hurt as Jesus would.
- Read (or better yet, know) some words from God's Word that will help each of you size up the situation and determine what should be done about it.
- Pray together, not so much that the problem will go away, but that growth and wholeness will come to everyone involved. Pray in love for the hurtful person.

- Find creative ways as a family and as individuals to channel energies that might otherwise have been wasted on hatred, resentments, and bitterness.
- Thank God for the experience, and return good for evil. Here are some helpful resources from God's Word to help in your relationships:

"Children, obey your parents in the Lord; for this is right. Honour thy father and mother; which is the first commandment with promise. That it may be well with thee, and thou mayest live long on the earth" (Eph. 6:1–3 KJV).

"Our bodies are composed of many parts and all the parts are needed to form a complete body" 1 Cor. 12:12 TLB).

"Don't be anxious about tomorrow. God will take care of your tomorrow too. Live one day at a time" (Matt. 6:34 TLB).

"Don't criticize, and then you won't be criticized. For others will treat you as you treat them" (Matt. 7:1-2 TLB).

"Let the little children come to me. Don't stop them" (Matt. 19:14).

"Blessed are the peacemakers: for they shall be called the children of God" (Matt. 5:9 KJV).

"Don't worry about things—food, drink, and clothes. Look at the field lilies! They don't worry. If God cares so wonderfully for flowers won't He more surely care for you?" (Matt. 6:25–30 TLB).

"Little children, let us stop just saying we love people; let us really love them, and show it by our actions" (1 John 3:18 TLB).

"Love your enemies, do good to them which hate you" (Luke 6:27-31 KJV).

The Love Chapter, 1 Corinthians 13, is really good for helping us see what kind of attitude we should have about winning and losing, giving and taking, and all things in loving as Jesus would.

"Whoever wants to save his life will lose it" (Matt. 16:25 NIV).

(The Living Bible translation of 1 John is excellent for family relationships, it's all about loving each other and showing it.)

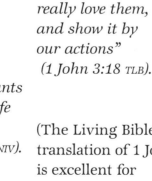

teachable moments

A Father Remembered

As the mother of four children, ages fifteen, thirteen, ten, and eight, I approached the first anniversary of my husband's death with some real soul-searching. I had been praying and asking God what I should do that would be meaningful and draw us all closer to Him. I believe God gave me a creative plan to commemorate this special day for our family.

In God's timing, the day before the anniversary of my husband's death, I had to attend a graveside memorial service for a friend. As I stood there God spoke to me, "You can have a graveside service too," He said. After more prayer here is what we did:

- Prepared an order of service.
- Asked everyone to set aside the date as a special family day.
- Gathered needed materials: Daddy's Bible, cleaning equipment for the headstone, individually wrapped flowers, blankets to sit on, pads of paper, pencils, and song sheets.

Our Anniversary Graveside Service

As we cleaned the headstone and then sat on the blankets, I asked my oldest child, Janell, to read Mark 16:2–7 about the resurrection. We then sang "Thy Word Is a Lamp Unto My Feet." I read a story about a man who was walking through the cemetery, looking at headstones and wondering what people would remember about him when he was gone. I then handed each child a pad of paper and asked them to answer two questions: What do you wish other people could know about your dad? What are some good memories you have of your dad? I had to help my eight-year-old with some words, but even after ten minutes they all wanted to keep writing. We laughed and had a wonderful sharing time. As each one shared, we put a flower into a vase. I marveled at what God was doing in our midst. My son Daniel read Psalm 116:12–19, and we sang "Oh, Lord You have been good, You have been faithful . . . to every generation" and "With all my heart I want to love You, Lord." I finished by reading some of their daddy's favorite Bible passages: John 14:1–4 and 15:16–17.

There was real bonding of our family that day. Nobody else knew their dad as we had known him. We huddled together, delighting in our memories and giving thanks to the Lord.

—*Helen Lundgren, Pasadena, California*

the final passage

One of the most important but hardest passages any family goes through is a loved one's leaving this life through the doorway of death. If the person who dies knows Jesus, this is the best passage because afterward he or she lives with Jesus forever where there is no more death or sadness. But for the ones left behind, death can be hard.

All of us have questions about death and eternal life. Here are some verses your family can read and discuss together in answer to questions we all ask:

✳ What kind of body will we have since we don't take this one with us to heaven? (1 Cor. 15:35–58)

✳ How long does it take to get to where Jesus is after we die? (2 Cor. 5:6, 8)

✳ Does God love us if He takes our (grandpa, daddy, auntie) away? (Rom. 8:38-39)

✳ Will I ever get over this sadness I feel? Can any good come out of this pain? (Rom. 8:28)

✳ Does God care how I feel? (1 Cor. 10:13–14)

♥ Instead of sending flowers when someone you love dies, send a living shrub or a small flowering tree.

♥ Write a note to remind the family that as surely as we die we shall also live again. Tell them that every time the tree you sent bursts into bloom in the spring, they can remember that the person they loved is living joyfully with Jesus. And when the tree "goes to sleep" in the winter, it is not dead but merely resting for its passage into summer.

♥ *John 11:25 and 12:24–25 gives us some encouraging words from Jesus.*

201

entryway reminders

Have you ever counted how many times your family comes in and out of the driveway and doorway of your house? Here are some ways to remind your family to live out its commitment to keep God at the center of your everyday lives.

💜 Hang a wooden sign above your kitchen door with a blessing or an encouraging text printed on it.

💜 Build a gate frame over your driveway and hang a sign from it with chain so people who visit will know that God is honored at your house.

💜 Paint a message such as "Peace be unto you" or "Shalom" on your mailbox or its support post.

💜 Use cement paint to paint one word on each of the stepping stones to your front door to express a joyful greeting such as:

✳ enter with thanksgiving.[1]
✳ I come with joy.[2]
✳ I thank my God upon every remembrance of you.[3]
✳ Serve the Lord with gladness.[4]
✳ Go with God.[5]
✳ I bless your coming in and going out this day and forever.

💜 Make a "country"-design sign for your house number that also says "Bless this day!"

[1] Psalm 100:4 KJV [4] Psalm 100:2 KJV
[2] Romans 15:32 KJV [5] See John 1:1 KJV
[3] Philippians 1:3 KJV

write it in my room

Decorate a child's room (or another room in the house) with a biblical theme. Some examples might be:

- The Garden of Eden patio room
- Daniel in the lions' den
- Paul's sailing-adventures room
- Noah's ark
- Fruits of the Spirit kitchen
- Dorcas, the maker of purple
- The land of milk and honey
- The tent-dweller's room
- The desert room
- The Red Sea room
- The shepherd David's hillside room

mezuzah reminder

When God commanded the Israelites to write His commandments "on the doorposts," they took Him literally. As a reminder to keep God's commandments on a daily basis in their homes and with their family lives, they made brass holders to fasten to the door casings. Inside, rolled up like a tiny scroll, was a parchment where the verses from Deuteronomy 6:4–9 and 11:13–21 were written in twenty-two lines. As the members of the family went in or out of the door, they touched or kissed the "mezuzah" and thought about their commitment to "Love the LORD your God with all your heart, with all your soul, and with all your might" (Deut. 6:5 NKJV). This is a great idea for any family who takes God's commandments seriously.

Mezuzahs can be bought at some religious bookstores, at Jewish shops, or ordered by mail from *The Source for Everything Jewish* (1-800-426-2567).

1 Type or write the words from Deuteronomy 6:4–9 and 11:13–21.

2 Roll up the paper lightly and slip it into the tiny holder.

3 Attach the mezuzah with screws to the doorframe of your house on the most-used entry.

4 Talk about these words together and about how your family can honor God with every aspect of your lives.

to make a mezuzah

The word *mezuzah* means "doorpost" and refers to Deuteronomy 6:9 and 11:20. It consists of a container of wood, metal, stone, clay, or paper containing a parchment lettered with Deuteronomy 6:4–9 and 11:13–21. The container has a hole through which one can see the word *Shaddai* which means "guardian of the doors of Israel."

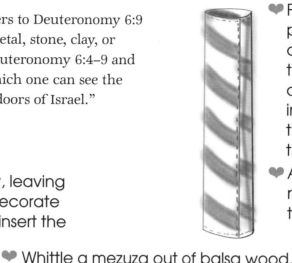

💜 Fold a rectangular piece of oilcloth or plastic cloth lengthwise. Turn it inside out then sew a long seam opposite the fold. Turn the "tube" to right-side out. Fold or sew the bottom, then insert the parchment and sew or fold the top. Use two tacks to attach it to the doorpost.

💜 Attach the *mezuzah* to the right side on the upper third of the doorpost.

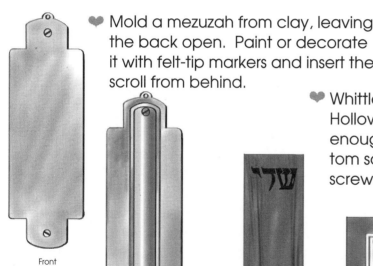

💜 Mold a mezuzah from clay, leaving the back open. Paint or decorate it with felt-tip markers and insert the scroll from behind.

Front

Back

💜 Whittle a mezuza out of balsa wood. Hollow out the center part but leave enough solid wood at the top and bottom so you can drive two nails or insert screws to hold it to the doorframe.

Front

Back

💜 Use a plastic toothbrush holder that has a hole in the top through which a screw can be driven.

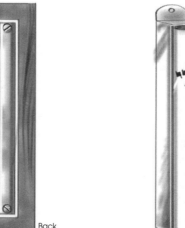

Arts and Crafts the Year Round, Vol. 2 (United Synagogue Community on Jewish Education, New York, 1965). p. 96-103 for more suggestions for making mezuzah containers.

You, your children, and grandchildren
must respect the LORD your God as
long as you live.
Obey all his rules and commands I give you
so that you will live a long time.

Deuteronomy 6:2

Section

14

promises TO PARENTS AND CHILDREN

❤ Proverbs 22:6 KJV

Train up a child in the way he should go: and when he is old, he will not depart from it.

❤ Isaiah 54:13 KJV

And all thy children shall be taught of the LORD; and great shall be the peace of thy children.

❤ 2 Timothy 3:14–15

But you should continue following the teachings you learned. You know they are true, because you trust those who taught you. Since you were a child you have known the Holy Scriptures which are able to make you wise. And that wisdom leads to salvation through faith in Christ Jesus.

❤ Ephesians 6:1–3 KJV

Children, obey your parents in the LORD: for this is right. Honour thy father and mother; which is the first commandment with promise; that it may be well with thee, and thou mayest live long on the earth.

❤ Ephesians 6:4 KJV

Fathers, provoke not your children to wrath: but bring them up in the nurture and admonition of the Lord.

❤ Isaiah 11:9 KJV

They shall not hurt nor destroy in all my holy mountain; for the earth shall be full of the knowledge of the LORD, as the waters cover the sea.

❤ Proverbs 20:11

Even children are known by their behavior; their actions show if they are innocent and good.

❤ Isaiah 11:6

Then wolves will live in peace with lambs, and leopards will lie down to rest with goats. Calves, lions, and young bulls will eat together, and a little child shall lead them.

❤ Jeremiah 1:4–8

The LORD spoke his word to me, saying: "Before I made you in your mother's womb, I chose you. Before you were born, I set you apart for a special work. I appoint you as a prophet to the nations." Then I said, "But Lord GOD, I don't know how to speak. I am only a boy." But the LORD said to me, "Don't say, 'I am only a boy.' You must go everywhere I send you, and you must say everything I tell you to say. Don't be afraid of anyone, because I am with you to protect you," says the LORD.

❤ Jeremiah 33:3 NIV

Call to me and I will answer you and tell you great and unsearchable things you do not know.

❤ John 6:35 NKJV
I am the bread of life. He who comes to Me shall never hunger.

❤ Hebrews 13:5 KJV
I will never leave thee, nor forsake thee.

❤ Deuteronomy 31:6 NIV
Be strong and courageous. Do not be afraid or terrified because of them (your enemies), for the LORD your God goes with you; he will never leave you nor forsake you.

❤ John 8:12
I am the light of the world. The person who follows Me will never live in darkness.

❤ John 14:6
I am the way, and the truth, and the life.

❤ John 11:25–26 NIV
I am the resurrection and the life.
He who believes in me will live, even though he dies; and whoever lives and believes in me will never die.

❤ Matthew 19:30 KJV
Many that are first shall be last; and the last shall be first.

❤ Ecclesiastes 11:1 NKJV
Cast your bread upon the waters, for you will find it after many days.

❤ Revelation 3:20 KJV
Behold, I stand at the door, and knock: if any man hears my voice, and opens the door, I will come in to him, and will sup with him, and he with me.

❤ Matthew 7:7 KJV
Ask, and it shall be given you; seek, and ye shall find; knock, and it shall be open to you.

❤ Romans 8:28 KJV
And we know that all things work together for good to them that love God, to them who are the called according to his purpose.

*"Teach them to
your children,
And talk about them
When you sit at home*

And walk along the road

When you lie down

And when you get up

Section

15

A Church in the Wild Woods

Does your family like to camp? Well, mine sure did. I should say my father did. At least, I think he did. Actually, I learned later in life that it wasn't that my parents liked to camp so much; it was that we didn't have enough money for motels. (I also thought my mom just liked picnics!)

Anyway, every time we arrived at a new campsite, we kids had a very important job to do. We had to scout out the area for just the right spot to have church. Since our parents had agreed to meet anywhere we selected, we took our responsibility very seriously. It had to be the most beautiful, most inspirational, most adventurous spot in the whole territory.

We rarely failed to satisfy our own expectations (or those of our parents). We had church in caves way up the sides of purple mountains. We had church on huge logs extending over rushing white rapids. We crossed pastures to meet near herds of cows and found ripe blackberry patches where we could snack during worship.

The curious thing was that while we thought we were leading our parents on a wild-goose chase to far-off places, we were always eager to have church while we were out camping. There was none of this, "Oh, no, why do we have to have church on our vacation?" No, when we all got in semi-comfortable seats and Dad began to read from the Bible, the nature surrounding us became holier. And when Mom started a song in her low alto voice, the streams and birds seemed to join us in worship. The wind and the swaying trees echoed God's majesty.

Each spot was somehow anointed. It was always perfect. Our parents praised us for picking such a special place to worship. Sometimes we camped with family friends. Then we had to show other kids how to pick out the spot. They would say, "Wait a minute. My mom will never climb up there!" But when it came time for church, everyone always did.

I'm glad I have worshiped in some of the most beautiful sanctuaries in the world . . . while sleeping in a tent!

Shout aloud, O earth beneath.
Burst into song,
you mountains, you forests,
and all you trees.
—paraphrase of Isaiah 44:23

 *Pat Verbal* —*Children's Minister, speaker, author, wife, and mother.*

Growing up, some of my fondest memories included hearing my mother sing Scripture songs to me, and also learning Bible trivia via different games involving family competition.

One of our favorite games, played while traveling in the car, consisted of Mom opening up the Bible and letting her finger fall randomly on any verse of Scripture. As she read the verses, we would all try to guess which book of the Bible she was reading from. We got a point for being the first one with the right answer, and whoever scored five points first, won the game. We could guess as often as we wanted, but we got a negative point for each wrong guess. Of course, the real object of the game was to try and beat Daddy!

Now that I'm an adult, I greatly enjoy teaching my own children Bible trivia and Scripture songs. Even when they were as young as four years old, they could quote all of Psalm 34. When I realized that my four year old could sing all of the commercial jingles, I knew she could also learn Scripture verses. I just needed to teach her in a way that would catch and sustain her interest.

I decided to pay attention to the fact that advertisers are well aware of: memory retention greatly increases when words are put to a tune or a rhythm.

Now I'm not a composer, but my kids didn't care as long as the songs were fun for them to sing. Many times, I have put Scripture verses to tunes my kids were already familiar with, such as "The Beverly Hillbillies," "Take Me Out to the Ball Game," etc. I would try to make sure that the tune fit the mood of the verse. For instance, last year the girls memorized Hebrews 11 all put to music. Toward the beginning of the chapter the song I used was very lighthearted and fun. Then, all of the sudden, the Bible verses began to talk about people being beaten and tortured for their faith. I had to work on it, but eventually I was able to make the music fit the mood of the Scripture.

Sometimes, I also have to really work at making the verse fit in with the rhythm of the song. Sound effects and hand motions greatly enhance the learning process. We have howled like dogs, roared like lions, and have also incorporated other assorted sound effects as we have learned Scripture. The crazier I made the songs, the more the children loved them.

One of my greatest joys is to pass by my children's rooms when they don't know I'm listening and hear them singing the Scripture verses that I have put to music and rhythm. I hope they'll pass this legacy on to their children just as my parents have passed it on to me.

 *Janice Edmonton* —*Wife, mother, and daughter of Dr. and Mrs. Adrian Rogers.*

A special event in our family's life that taught us the importance of the Bible principle, "*you have not because you ask not*" (James 4:2) occurred during a family vacation to the Grand Canyon. In our haste to go, I forgot to make a hotel reservation. When we arrived, all the hotels were filled and the nearest available hotel space was one and one-half hours away. We had been traveling all day and were hot, tired, sweaty, and frustrated. I was downright mad.

After receiving the bad news, we sat down to eat in the hotel restaurant to catch our breath. I wasn't a very good illustration of spiritual leadership during this time. My youngest daughter, Priscilla, looked up at me and said, "Dad, you know we haven't prayed about a hotel room."

Well, we had already been turned away and many others also before us, so I wasn't in a praying mood. I told her, very curtly, "You pray."

In simple, childlike faith, she said, "Lord, You know we have traveled a very long way to get here, and we are tired. They say that there are no rooms available, but we know you can get us a room, so please give us a room so we won't have to drive a long way to find another hotel. Thank You, in Jesus' name. Amen."

After she finished, I thought, *Now let's get back to the real world. Hurry up and eat so we can get on the road and find a hotel.*

While in this state of carnality, a gentleman came over to our table and said, "Aren't you the family who was looking for a room here?" I said, "Yes." He said, "I'm the manager, and a couple had an emergency and had to leave so we now have a room available if you still need it. The people who were in line in front of you aren't around, so it's yours if you want it."

All of a sudden, I started sounding spiritual again praising the Lord for answered prayer. Our family has never forgotten the lesson that God is concerned about hotel rooms for His children.

 *Tony Evans* —*Minister, author, husband, and father.*

I firmly believe that what we write on the heart of a child is indelible, and teaching them to hide God's word in their heart is one way to insure that it will always be a part of them.

Psalm 119:130 *"The entrance of thy word bringeth light"* was a verse which has specific blessing for me.

We had these words on a plaque in my home as I grew up and I taught it, along with others to my children. Sometimes they learned the Scriptures in songs. We would often sing them in the car as we traveled around, and many times I remember them repeating them on their way to school, or learning them in summer Bible school.

When my son, who had disowned us, changed his name and said he never wanted to see us again . . . leaving us for an alternate lifestyle, he told me recently (after his restoration to us and to the Lord) that he would wake up in the middle of the night when he was out there in that life, and would think of that particular verse and say to himself . . . . "Where is that light? There is no light in my life"— and that verse would flood back in his memory. It was that verse he had learned so many years before which brought conviction to him, and in turn, that brought him back to us asking forgiveness for his sin. This restoration came from the prompting of the Lord through the early verses he had memorized as a child.

My father, who was a minister, firmly believed that children should learn the Scriptures by heart and would have me in the car many times reciting verses over and over as a way of training. He had a class for young people on Scripture memorization and was determined that I, being his child, would be the star of the class.

I can remember having verses typed out on cards in the bathroom, in the kitchen on cupboards, and even once a verse was taped to my bicycle handles so I could learn on the way to school. Not only was the verse to be learned, but the "address" of it also.

We only had the King James version of the Bible then, so there was no way to change the words to fit another version.

The verse in Proverbs 13:12 says, *"Hope deferred makes the heart sick: but when dreams come true at last there is life and joy."*

I had learned that verse as a child when I didn't even *know* what the word deferred was, and a dream to me was riding my bike forever in the breeze. But as I matured and learned how we can be living in that "hope deferred" time . . . when our dreams are not coming true, and our children may have gone off on a detour in life, we are living in that parenthesis— waiting for God to knock out the end of it—and then finally we have that dream come true. One version (NIV) says "but a longing fulfilled is a tree of life." This verse gives us hope that although we may be living in that hope-deferred time in our life, it will not last forever—it will pass, and we will have that hope and joy—a tree of life.

 *Barbara Johnson* —*Humorist, author and speaker, wife, mother, and Founder of Spatula Ministries.*

In the springtime seven years ago, my husband passed away after a long illness. Needless to say, his death had a profound impact on me and our five children, but it has also made an impression on our thirteen grandchildren, including the eight that have been born since he died.

I believed then, and I still believe now, that it is important for the grandchildren to hear plenty of stories about Papa and to look at him in family photographs in the hope that they might come to know him in some small way. If only through the collective memory of those of us who knew him. So whenever my grandchildren are with me, the stories of Papa and his life here and his new home there are often part of our conversation. I will sometimes say to one of them, "I wonder what Papa is going to do today?" And together we try and imagine what he might be doing today in his new home.

Two of my grandchildren stay with me while their father is at work. One morning as they were getting ready for school. I said to Grant, my blond-haired, cherub-faced, five-year-old grandson. "My, my, you do look great this morning!"

He took a deep breath, squared his shoulders, and looked at himself in the mirror.

With no small measure of pride he gave out one of those grins that only he can give and said, "Yep, I do, don't I? I think I'm about ready to die."

In astonishment I said, "Grant, why did you say that?"

"Well," he said, "if I die, I'll go to heaven and I'll get to see Jesus and then I'll get to see Papa. Papa didn't get to know me but I think he is really going to like me."

Grant is right, of course—Papa is going to like him, very much if I know Papa at all. But Grant is right about another thing too.

God loved us so much He gave His most precious gift so that we might know Jesus personally and go to heaven and spend forever with the Father and the Son and, of course, with Papa and all the others who have gone before. Our work on this earth is simply to love the Father with our whole heart, to show His love to others, and to learn to listen for His voice in all that happens in our lives. To listen for that voice in the confident, curious wisdom of the little ones among us, in the memories and stories of our lives, and, yes, even in the death of the ones we love.

 *Peggy Benson*—*author, conference-and-retreat speaker, mother of five, and grandmother of thirteen.*

When our children were small, Peggy and I would often take them to visit elderly people. We felt it was good for them as well for the elderly folks we visited. We did this almost weekly, and we encouraged the elderly people to tell stories about when they were young. Our children, in turn, were absolutely fascinated by the stories of what it was like "back then." We encouraged the children to do something special during each of the visits. Sometimes they were asked to memorize a Bible verse, other times to sing a song, or to bring a drawing they made in Sunday School.

In the midst of all of this we were quick to point out to them the teachings of Scripture. *"This is true religion to visit the fatherless and the widows in their affliction and to keep oneself spotless from the world" (James 1:27).*

Tony Campolo
—Author, international speaker, sociologist, husband, father of two, and grandfather of two.

My mother always encouraged my sisters, brother, and me to memorize Scripture. In fact, she did more than encourage, she gave us an incentive to want to learn it quickly. Usually on Sunday afternoons before we could go out and play she would give us a verse to memorize. As soon as we were able to commit it to memory, we were free to go out and play. She always made it fun for us so that we would want to know the word of God.

One particular verse that comes quickly to mind is Proverbs 1:10, *"My son, if sinners entice thee consent thou not."* Mother always paraphrased so that we could grasp its meaning . . . . *"My son, if bad boys tell you to do bad things, say NO."*

Growing up there were always temptations in school. Buddies would try to lead me astray. I have seen this with my own children. Having four kids of my own, I have tried to instill in them the importance of Scripture memory. Proverbs 1:10 is one that I have also emphasized. As a young person it is very easy to get pulled into the wrong things. Even as an adult, this verse continually comes to mind and serves as a reminder to stay focused on the Lord and not let peer pressure win my attention. Learning to say "no" keeps one's eyes focused on the cross of Christ. There is strength that comes from saying "no" and after the first experience, God uses it to guide and direct which makes it easier to say "no" the second and third time.

Franklin Graham
—President of Samaritan's Purse, husband, father of four, and son of Billy Graham.

"Talk about them when you sit at home . . ."

Never have I been more convinced of the Bible's relevance to our everyday world than the year our sons, Andy and Curtis, were eight and ten years old. That was the year of the "Bible Supper Club." Each boy invited a friend to take part in a weekly, Tuesday after-school time of play, Bible study, and supper at our house.

"Please, Lord," I prayed as I began to prepare for our first meeting. "Help me find a topic that four energetic, live-wires will find relevant and exciting."

Curtis' assignment for his Current Events class was the answer to my prayer. The students were to bring in articles about the biggest news story of the day, the U.S. hostages in Iran. I immediately saw the connection between that current-day crisis and the exciting, ancient tale of Daniel and his friends being held hostage in Babylonia, told in the Book of Daniel.

Every Tuesday after school my foursome would arrive (Curtis, Andy, and their friends Eric and Brett.) After a snack and a couple of hours of play in the neighborhood, they would gather around our dining table for their Bible adventure. I challenged the boys to imagine themselves held captive and far away from home. I had them write to their families as though they were hostages. We talked about the kind of courage and comfort and guidance that Daniel and his friends received from God, and its present-day availability to believers. They were especially impressed with Daniel's health food diet and with his bold defiance of his captors.

Of course the boys' favorite feature of the Bible Supper Club was the supper itself, which usually consisted of Pizza or hamburgers and lots of cupcakes for dessert.

My children are grown now. Andy is a youth pastor and Curt teaches in a Christian school. I am constantly impressed with the creative ways they come up with to present the Bible to the kids they teach. And I have noticed that neither one is above using pizza and cupcakes for bait!

Claire Cloninger—Author, *lyricist, speaker, wife, and mother.*

Every August we vacation with our family in the mountains of North Carolina. We introduced hiking to our children at an early age and now they seem to love it as much as we do. Being surrounded with the beauty and majesty of the mountains seemed to stir within each one of us a renewed sense of our loving Creator who would design something so wonderful for us to enjoy. It is easy to talk about the awesomeness of God on these hikes.

Another benefit to hiking together has been to reinforce Scripture through actual experiences. Our favorite example was one summer when our oldest had just turned six and we had a long uphill hike back to our destination after lunch. It wasn't easy for her little legs to keep going but she kept hiking and started talking about one of her "G.T. and the Halo Express" tapes. It was the one on Hebrews 12:1–3, about running the race that is set before us with endurance. She suddenly understood what it meant to persevere—"Keep on keeping on"—in order to not grow weary and lose heart on the hike or in her walk as a Christian. She actually saw that perseverance had a reward because at the end of the hike she had a sense of pride in finishing it on her own just as we who persevere as Christians will receive the reward of eternity as well as developing a character that will be more pleasing to God.

Now whether we may be on a difficult hike or facing a challenge at home or school, we smile and say that "we need to persevere and just keep on keeping on."

 *Elizabeth Robinson* —*Wife, mother, and daughter of Pat and DeDe Robertson.*

My mother was a high school English teacher whose joyous enthusiasm for learning was contagious. She believed her four children should be served a "smattering" of Shakespeare, world history, down-home humor and the holy Scriptures along with their evening meals. The memorization and integration of God's Word into our daily life routine was part of her life mission. Often, she would write a scripture verse on the 6' x 8' chalkboard mounted on our kitchen wall and simply notify the household that no one would be admitted to the evening meal who could not recite it letter-perfect from memory. More often, she found a more palatable (if bizarre) way to ingrain such knowledge in our young minds. Any zany little left turn of everyday life seemed to spark or connect to a spiritual idea! Quoting Scripture, teaching scriptural principles, sharing biblical thoughts and ideas with her children came as naturally as smiling at them.

When I was about twelve, Mom and I painted a room together—she was high on a ladder, putting a second coat on the ceiling moulding; I diligently labored on the baseboards. It was quiet except for the sibilant swish and swash of the brushes. Suddenly we, at once, became aware that the other had stopped and I turned around to find her looking down, pensively posed, chin in hand.

"Whatcha' thinking?" she asked.

"Oh, I don't know—Just restin' I guess—wishin' we were through with this job. What's on your mind?"

"I was watching you and being glad I wasn't here doing this alone—feeling thankful that I have you for a daughter."

I looked up at her. "Well, your thoughts are loftier than mine!" I giggled proudly at my clever *double entendre*. She laughed appreciatively, then dramatically delivered, with characteristic gusto and animation, her next thought sequence:

"'*My thoughts are not your thoughts, neither are your ways my ways,' declares the Lord. 'As the heavens are higher than the earth, so are my ways higher than your ways and my thoughts than your thoughts.'* He isn't 'uppity' about it . . . He's just God!"

We chuckled together, both of us taking in the message and the cherished moment; then once again, the room fell silent, except for the swishing brushes.

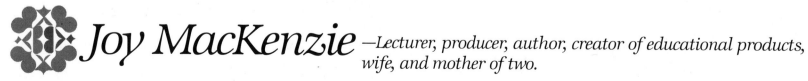

Joy MacKenzie —*Lecturer, producer, author, creator of educational products, wife, and mother of two.*

When our girls were young, we as a family, chose from the Book of Proverbs, The Living Bible paraphrase, a verse that would be a "watchword" for each of the four of us. The Scripture related directly to some life habit or pattern that needed to be addressed.

Kristen's watchword was Proverbs 15:15: *"When a man is gloomy, everything seems to go wrong. When he is cheerful, everything seems right."* Kris was not a morning person, and these words *sometimes* eased the "getting-up grumps!"

Shana was at an age where she found comfort in Proverbs 29:25: *"Fear of man is a dangerous trap, but to trust in God means safety!"*

Mom, the obsessive-compulsive, teacher-mother-homemaker often needed to be reminded that *"A relaxed attitude lengthens a woman's life."* (Proverbs 14:30), and Proverbs 24:3–4 provided good advice for me, the "flexible," wing-it type: *"Any enterprise is built by wise planning, becomes strong through common sense, and profits wonderfully by keeping abreast of the facts."*

The four passages were copied with colored marker on construction paper and mounted on the kitchen wall, where they remained for several weeks and were often quoted as "watchwords" at an appropriate moment.

Years later, all of us can still quote all four verses!

Bob MacKenzie
—Entrepreneur in Christian music business, married to Joy MacKenzie, and father of two.

Erin Olivia Greene is our five-year-old daughter—sweet, strong-willed, pretty, impetuous, and full of energy. She's usually the first one up in the morning at our house and knows that if she persists I'll finally get out of bed and join her for a Bible story.

First we head downstairs to the kitchen where I pour orange juice for Erin and a much needed cup of coffee for me. Within a few minutes we're seated on the couch with Erin's Bible, a condensed illustrated children's version. I read and she looks at the pictures.

It's been two years now that we've enjoyed this morning ritual together. By now Erin is familiar with countless characters and stories from the Bible; her favorites are Ruth, Moses, Mary, Martha, and Jesus. I believe that God is using it to bring Erin to a better and better knowledge of Him and His love for her.

Just as importantly, I'm learning how to pass along a spiritual heritage to those God has entrusted to me. What a privilege to share God's story with our children. It brings great joy and satisfaction to this father's heart.

"He who fears the Lord has a secure fortress, and for his children it will be a refuge" (Proverbs 14:26).

Buddy Greene
—Christian musician, husband, and father of two.

Come springtime, when I'm out planting beds and filling pots with blooming things, my children begin to get interested in flowers. So this year, we made our own pot of unique flowers; we call them our Spiritual Garden. We have a big terra-cotta flowerpot on our kitchen table, filled with peat moss, into which we stick brightly colored construction-paper flowers with popsicle-stick stems. On the flowers we write Scripture verses that we have learned at Sunday School or have read together in the Bible. The more we pray, the more we grow and learn, the more our Spiritual Garden blooms!

Some of our Scripture flowers include Ephesians 6:1 (Children obey your parents, for this is right.), John 13:35 (Love one another.), and, that real sticky one, Ephesians 4:32 (Be kind one to another, tenderhearted, forgiving each other, even as God forgives you.) We have three boys, ages nine, three, and one, so we run up against that "forgiveness" thing quite often. Just the other day, I had to interrupt a shouting match between the older two brothers. Neither was being kind, and neither wanted to forgive. I sat them down at the kitchen table, and that Scripture flower caught my eye. I plucked it from the pot and handed it over to Seth, my fourth-grader, who read it with a grimace and was about to stick it back in the pot, when I stopped him.

"I don't think that belongs in our garden," I said. "There's not much kindness or forgiveness growing around here. And while we're at it," I added, pulling flowers from the pot, "let's take out this one about loving one another, and about honoring each member, and . . ."

"Mom! Stop it!" they wailed. "You're yanking out all the flowers! Now it's ugly!"

And so are our hearts, and our family life, without kindness and forgiveness and love growing between brothers. We put the flowers back, one by one, and we talked about how our Spiritual Garden is more than just showy flowers in a pot. It's real things like sharing and speaking kindly, like giving the other one first turn and not losing our tempers—it's those qualities that have to take root and grow in our hearts before we can have a home where God's Word is alive and in full bloom.

♥

My fourth-grader, Seth, is a writer. He loves to make up stories, poems, songs . . . just about anything. I have discovered that a great way to get him to make the truth of a Scripture real to him is to let him put it in his own words, creatively. "His own words" can be both entertaining (in "God's Top Ten," the Ten Commandments, "Honor thy father and mother "becomes "Don't 'dis' your parents") and surprisingly poignant. My favorite is Seth's rap song about the Golden Rule: "Treat Your Friends (Just Like You Want To Be Treated)." Seth made a tape of several of his songs, and now he can rap to the Truth in his own words.

♥

When a student who is special to me, like my nephew most recently, enters his senior year in high school, I begin working on his graduation gift. I buy a new Bible, and I read it through for him all year, highlighting passages and making notes in the margins next to Scriptures that I know he will really need in his new life after graduation. It's a great way for me to read the Bible through, and when he goes off to college, he has a very personalized Bible to turn to when he feels alone and overwhelmed.

Karla Worley —*Christian singer, author, wife, and mother of two.*

A tradition that I started several years ago was to get alone with God on New Year's Day (or at least within the first two weeks of January). During that time I would write down the many answers to prayer for our family and those close to us. I would also write out our prayer concerns for the upcoming year.

After concluding the prayer section, I pray for the members of the immediate family and ask God for a special Scripture for each one. I give them to my husband and children and talk to them about what God might be saying. We review them at different times throughout the year and again pray that God would minister them to our hearts.

On New Year's Eve we have a candlelight dinner, share God's Word, His blessings and answers to prayers. This year, we asked the children to ask God for a Scripture to share with the family. We were thrilled and surprised to see what words God had led them to and how appropriately they ministered to the family.

As a result of this tradition, I have a wonderful record of God's words and work in my family throughout the early years of our children's lives, and a significant account of how the Lord is speaking to us.

❤

"Be anxious for nothing, but in everything by prayer and petition, with thanksgiving present your requests to God. And the peace that transcends all understanding, will guard your hearts and minds in Christ Jesus" (Philippians 4:6–7).

As the children get older, I have discovered how easy it is for Tim and me to pray *for* them instead of letting them learn about the power of an individual relationship between each child and Almighty God. By doing this, we may be stunting their discovery of the intimacy of God in their lives. Children often assume that if *we* pray for them, then God is certain to hear. Parents might presume that they know how to cover a topic more thoroughly than the child. The Lord wants His children—of all ages—to come to Him all the time.

My daughter, Elizabeth, wanted me to teach her Vacation Bible School class. The space I had signed up for was filled and there seemed to be no possibility for change. Elizabeth and her best friend got busy, took their disappointment to their Heavenly Father and shortly before the start of camp, I was asked to teach her section, accompanied by her best friend's mother.

Since that time, she has no hesitation in taking her needs to God and He answers her magnificently.

We must teach our children not only to pray for themselves but for us, too, as we struggle through the challenges of being their parents. What a relief for them to know that *we* are in God's hands too.

❤

Lisa Robertson—Wife, mother, and daughter-in-law of Pat and DeDe Robertson.

Write them down

*And tie them
on your hands as a sign.
Tie them on your forehead
to remind you*

And write them on your doors
And gates."

Deuteronomy 6:7–8

Section **16**

resources for hiding the Word

225

Bible music for kids

Baby Bible Promises
Bible stories and Scripture verses
for parent and children set to
quiet music. Brentwood Music,
Brentwood, Tennessee.

Bible Play Along Series
Fully dramatized story cassettes
to bring Bible stories to life. Can
be used with Bible Greats Play
Sets and Action Figures. Rainfall,
Grand Rapids, Michigan.

Bible Stories about Kids Series
Tape-and -book sets to hear, read,
sing, and color along with.

Dear God Series
Songs, rhymes, and Scripture
verses talk about Jesus and kids.
Word, Dallas, Texas.

Hide 'Em in Your Heart,
vol. 1 and 2, by Green. Bible
memory favorites book and tape.
Sparrow, Brentwood, Tennessee.

My Bible Stories
Concordia Publishing House,
Saint Louis, Missouri.

Integrity Music Just for Kids Series
Songs that teach, songs that
praise. Integrity Hosanna Music,
distributed by Sparrow,
Brentwood, Tennessee.

Kids Sing Praise, vol. 1, 2, and 3
Praise, Scripture, and sing-along
songs for kids (book available).
Brentwood Music, Brentwood,
Tennessee.

Little Saints in Praise
by Richard and Elaine Osborne.
Word, Dallas, Texas.

The Singing Bible
by Richard and Elaine Osborne.
Word, Dallas, Texas.

My First Bible in Songs
by Kenneth Taylor (narrated by
Mark Taylor). Tyndale House,
Wheaton, Illinois.

My First Bible in Songs
by Mark Taylor. (A mini-book
and audio cassette, ages 2-6).
Tyndale House,
Wheaton, Illinois.

This Is Our Father's World:
A Kid's ABC of Ecology. A fun
collection of songs on split trax to
help kids understand their biblical
responsibility to take care of God's
creation. Brentwood Music,
Brentwood, Tennessee.

Bible music for adults

Integrity Hosanna Music Series
Distributed by Sparrow,
Brentwood, Tennessee.

Praise Series
The Maranatha! Singer. A series of
fifteen titles of praise music set to the
praise of the Scripture. Maranatha
Music, Louisville, Kentucky.

Praise and Worship Series
Word, Dallas, Texas.

Scripture Memory Song Series
Contemporary music teaching God's
Word. Distributed by Sparrow,
Brentwood, Tennessee.

Scripture Music Nature Series
Inspiring Scripture set to peaceful
music to soothe your spirit. Thomas
Nelson, Nashville, Tennessee.

Spirit Song Series
Diadem, Chatham, Illinois.

Vineyard Psalms, vol. 1 and 2
Vineyard Ministries International,
Anaheim, California.

Worship Alive Series
Outstanding songs of scriptural
praise and worship that have become standards. Star Song,
Nashville, Tennessee.

Bible games, puzzles, & activity books

Activity Resource Books
Graded-activities book series for elementary ages. Standard Publishing, Cincinnati, Ohio.

Bible Buddies
Players begin in the Garden of Eden and adventure through biblical history to Noah's Ark, David and Goliath, parting of the Red Sea, and more. Two or more players, ages seven and up. Scarborough, Ontario, Canada.

Bible Checkers
Warner Press, Anderson, Indiana.

Bible Drills and Quizzes
(ages six through twelve). Rainbow Books, San Diego, California.

Bible Crafts
(graded series). Rainbow Books, San Diego, California.

Bible Games
(graded series). Rainbow Books, San Diego, California.

Bible Puzzles (series)
Rainbow Books, San Diego, California.

Bible Stories about Jesus
(graded-activities book series). Rainbow Books, San Diego, California.

Bible Story Puzzle Series
(ages five through eleven). Shining Star Publishers, Carthage, Illinois.

The Bible Tells Me So
Gold 'n' Honey Book, Questar Publishers, Sisters, Oregon.

Bible Time Puzzle Series
(reproducible pages for ages three through six). Shining Star Publications, Carthage, Illinois.

Bible Times Crafts for Kids
Gospel Light, Ventura, California.

The Complete Book of Bible Trivia
Tyndale House, Wheaton, Illinois.

Creative Bible Crafts
(graded series). Rainbow Books, San Diego, California.

Crossword Puzzles about the Old Testament
by Shirley Beegle. Warner Press, Anderson, Indiana.

Crossword Puzzles
Bible Characters from the Old Testament. Warner Press, Anderson, Indiana.

Favorite Bible Stories
(graded-activities series). Cut-Color-Paste series and Make-Color-Solve series. Rainbow Books, San Diego, California.

Find the Word Bible Puzzles
(series). by W. B. Freeman. Wisdom & Praise and Parables & Miracles. Standard Publishing, Cincinnati, Ohio.

Fun Stuff for Kids
by Michael Strefts. Zondervan, Grand Rapids, Michigan.

Life and Lessons of Jesus
A series of creative Bible learning activities for ages six through twelve by Tracy Laffingwell. Harrod. David C. Cook, Chicago, Illinois.

Nelson's Super Book of Bible Activities for Kids
by W. B. Freeman. Oliver Nelson, Nashville, Tennessee.

Nelson's Super Book of Bible Word Games Crosswords, scrambles, and many other word games. Books 1, 2, and 3. Oliver Nelson, Nashville, Tennessee.

NIV Bible Crosswords
Zondervan Press, Grand Rapids, Michigan.

Pict-o-Graph Redi-Cut Stories
Level 1 (ages two through five)
Level 2 (ages five through eight)
Level 3 (ages eight through twelve)
Level 4 (ages twelve and up).
Standard Publishing, Cincinnati, Ohio.

Planting Spiritual Seeds:
75 Nature Activities to Help Children and Youth Learn about God. by Judy Gattis Smith. Abingdon Press, Nashville, Tennessee.

Preschool Bible Crafts
by Kathy Darling. Shining Star, Carthage, Illinois.

Preschool Bible Learning Centers
by Ramona Warren. Shining Star Publishers, Carthage, Illinois.

Puzzles and Games Series
The Life of Jesus, The Teachings of Jesus, The Birth of the Church, The Journeys of Paul, Old Testament History, Bible Story Heros and Heroines. Standard Publishing, Cincinnati, Ohio.

Tyndale Crossword Puzzles Series
by Terry Hall. Tyndale House, Wheaton, Illinois.

Willmington's Book of Bible Lists
Tyndale House, Wheaton, Illinois.

Word Search—New Testament
Warner Press, Anderson, Indiana.

52 Games that Teach the Bible
For ages four through twelve. Rainbow Books, San Diego, California.

52 Ways to Teach Bible Reading
For ages four through twelve. Rainbow Books, San Diego, California.

52 Ways to Teach Memory Verses
For ages four through twelve. Rainbow Books, San Diego, California.

74 More Fun and Challenging Bible Crosswords
Tyndale House, Wheaton, Illinois.

78 Great Fun and Challenging Word Searches Tyndale House, Wheaton, Illinois.

101 Fun Bible Word Searches
Tyndale House, Wheaton, Illinois.

101 Bible Puzzles
(Reproducible), based on International Sunday School Lessons. Standard Publishing, Cincinnati, Ohio.

101 Fun Bible Crosswords
Tyndale House, Wheaton, Illinois.

Bible board & table games

Bible Fun and Activity Pack
A young reader's Christian Library Edition. Fun stuff for home and travel in a convenient carrying case.

The Bible Game
Tyndale House, Wheaton, Illinois.

Bible Games Chest
Warner Press, Anderson, Indiana.

Bible Treasure Hunt
Standard Publishing, Cincinnati, Ohio.

Bible Story Lotto
Standard Publishing, Cincinnati, Ohio.

Bible Story Picture Puzzles
Standard Publishing, Cincinnati, Ohio.

Bible Trivia
Shining Star, Carthage, Illinois.

Bible Warmups
Question cards with answer choices; body heat illuminates the answers when thumb is held against colored square. The series includes several different packs.

Bibleopoly
Starting "In the Beginning" you will journey through Bible cities, with suggestions for meditation and celebration.

The Great Cake Chase
Victor Books, Standard Publishing, Cincinnati, Ohio.

Inklings
Great for families, friends, and church groups. Players receive clues until they can guess answers. Sharpens Bible knowledge for ages eight through eighty-eight.

Kids' Bible Challenge Game
For two to four players ages six through twelve.
Rainfall Productions.

People and Places in the Book
Tyndale House, Wheaton, Illinois.

Bible skits & drama

Childhood Is a Stage:
Sketches & Monologues for Children by Martha Bolton. Lillinas, Kansas City, Missouri.

A Funny Thing Happened to Me on the Way Through the Bible
by Martha Bolton.
Lillinas, Kansas City, Missouri.

Let My People Laugh
by Martha Bolton.
Lillinas, Kansas City, Missouri.

Option Plays
by Chap Clark, Duffy Robbins, and Mike Yaconelli. Zondervan, Grand Rapids, Michigan.

Greatest Skits on Earth
by Wayne Rice and Mike Yoconelli. Zondervan, Grand Rapids, Michigan.

Acting Up Again: 13 Scripture Sketches by Doug Smee.
Lillinas, Kansas City, Missouri.

Fun Group-Involving Skits
by Linda Snyder, Tom Tozer, Amy Nappa. Group Publishing, Loveland, Colorado.

Characters: Comedies, Dramas, and Raps Featuring Bible Characters
by James and Lois Watkin.
Lillinas, Kansas City, Missouri.

Bible drills

Bible Blockbusters
by Cyril Barnes. Based on the
Central Independent Television
series. Harper Collins, New York.

1000 Bible Drill Questions
by W. Burgess McCreary. Warner
Press, Anderson, Indiana.

Bible helps

Davis's Dictionary of the Bible
by J. D. Davis. Helps any age get
more out of Bible Study.

All the Birds of the Bible
by Alice Parmalee. Keats Publishing,
New Canaan, Connecticut.

Bible Promises for Growing Christians
by James Ryan.

Bible Promises for Soul-Winners
by James Ryan.

The Complete Book of Bible Literacy
by Mark D. Taylor.
Tyndale House, Wheaton, Illinois.

videos and video games

Superbook Video Bible Twelve videos in the set.
This series plants two kids right in the middle of
Bible times for thrilling action in heartwarming
Bible stories.

Teenager, How Are You Going to Survive the 1990s?
Precept Ministries, Chattanooga, Tennessee.

The Wonders of Creations A three video boxed set.
A front-row seat for the greatest show in God's
universe. Includes: Planet Earth, Animal Kingdom,
and Human Life.

The Animated Stories from the New Testament
Twelve videos in the series.
Family Entertainment Network.

Lord, Is It Warfare? Teach Me to Stand
by Kay Arthur. Precept Ministries,
Chattanooga, Tennessee.

Sex, Dating, and Teens by Kay Arthur.
Precept Ministries, Chattanooga, Tennessee.

Exodus Video game with one hundred fast-paced
mazes and two hundred fifty Bible questions.
Wisdom Tree, Inc.

King of Kings Three video adventures on
one cartridge. Wisdom Tree, Inc.

Bibles for youth

The Adventure Bible
(New International Version). A study Bible for kids. Zondervan, Grand Rapids, Michigan.

The Answers
(New King James Version). Two hundred sixty writings by the world's best-known Christian authors examining issues and events of our time. This Bible for teenagers and adults will make God's Word relevant to your life situations.

The Toddler's Bible
by V. Gilbert Beers. Scripture Press, Wheaton, Illinois.

Bible for Today's Family
(Contemporary English Version). An understandable translation for the whole family. American Bible Society, New York.

The Children's Illustrated Bible
Stories retold by Selina Hastings and illustrated by Eric Thomas. Star Song Publishing Group, Nashville, Tennessee.

The Children's Living Bible
paraphrased by Kenneth Taylor and illustrated by Richard and Frances Hook. Tyndale House, Wheaton, Illinois.

Story of Stories
by Karen Hinckley. The Bible in narrative form adding context, cultural information, and chronology told with the flair of a master storyteller.

The Hosanna Bible
interpreted especially for preschool children. WordKids, Word, Dallas, Texas.

The King and the Beast
(Contemporary English Version). This New Testament for students is packed with hundreds of articles dealing with issues young people face.

The Lakeside Town series
Six Bible titles for toddlers. David C. Cook, Chicago, Illinois.

My First Bible in Pictures
by Mark Taylor. Tyndale House, Wheaton, Illinois.

Every Day With God:
A Child's Daily Bible (NCV) Word, Dallas, Texas.

One-Minute Bible for Kids
(New International Version). One-minute Scripture readings with facts and activities. Garborg Press, Bloomington, Minnesota.

One-Minute Bible for Students
(New International Version). For ages twelve through sixteen. Garborg Press, Bloomington, Minnesota.

Read with Me Bible
(New International Version). More than one hundred of the best-loved Bible stories for children ages four through ten. Zondervan Press, Grand Rapids, Michigan.

Bibles for Youth, *continued*

The Book for Children
by Kenneth Taylor. Tyndale
House, Wheaton, Illinois.

The Toddler's Activity Book
Thomas Nelson, Nashville,
Tennessee.

The Youth Bible
(New Century Version). Word,
Dallas, Texas.

The Words of Jesus
(King James Version). Arranged
and chronicled by Gilbert James
and Brett and Melbourne
Feltman. Consolidated Book
Publishers, Chicago, Illinois.

The Adventure Bible Handbook
Vander Maas, editor. A wild
and spectacular hi-tech trip
through the Bible for kids.
Zondervan,
Grand Rapids, Michigan.

Bibles especially for men and women

*The Bible Incorporated in Your Life,
Job, and Business* compiled by
Michael Q. Pink. Hidden Manna,
Mount Juliet, Tennessee.

The International Inductive Study Bible
(New American Standard Version).
Harvest House, Eugene, Oregon.

The Thompson Chained Reference Bible
(King James Version or New International Version). Absolutely the best
study, chained reference Bible with
excellent concordance, charts, maps,
outlined study of characters, and
analysis of books. B. B. Kirkbridge
Bible Co., Indianapolis, Indiana.

The Couple's Devotional Bible (New
International Version). With
devotions from many well-known
Christian couples integrated into
the text. Zondervan,
Grand Rapids, Michigan.

The Men's Devotional Bible
(New International Version). With
devotions from many well-known
Christian men integrated into the
text. Zondervan,
Grand Rapids, Michigan.

The Women's Devotional Bible (New
International Version). With devotions from many well-known
Christian women integrated into
the text. Zondervan,
Grand Rapids, Michigan.

Bible storybooks

The Story of Jesus
by Mary Bachelor. Lion Publishers, San Diego, California.

The Bible Discovery Series
Tyndale House, Wheaton, Illinois.

Bible Animals
by Barton, Guilvia, Kendricks, Lucas, Veerman and Wilson.

Bible Story Series: The Star of Creation, Noah's Ark, Jonah and the Big Fish, and The First Christmas Standard Publishing, Cincinnati, Ohio.

Children of the Bible
by Cindy Bow and Paul Brownlow. Brownlow Publishing, Fort Worth, Texas.

Stories Jesus Told
by Nick Butterworth and Mick Inkpen. Gold 'n' Honey Books. Questar Publishers, Sisters, Oregon.

The Parable of . . . Series
by Helen Caswell. Abingdon Press, Nashville, Tennessee.

Egermeier's Bible Story Book
by Elsie E. Egermeier. This is one of the best Bible story books for the whole family. Warner Press, Anderson, Indiana.

The Bible
by Chad Frye. A fully illustrated collection of Old and New Testament Bible stories, ideal for ages two through seven.

My Bible Stories
by Carol Green. Concordia Publishers, St. Louis, Missouri.

Jesus for Children
by William Griffin. Winston Press, Houston, Texas.

A Child's Book of Bible People
by Sheri Dunham Haan. Baker, Grand Rapids, Michigan.

365 Short Stories from the Bible
by Jesse Lyman Heirlbut. A short story from the Bible for each day of the year with discussion questions and drawings.

The Illustrated Children's Bible
Harcourt Brace, Orlando, Florida.

Little Butterfly Shape Book Series.
The qualities of a Christian. Chariot Books, a division of David C. Cook, Chicago, Illinois.

The Kingfisher's Children's Bible
by Ann Pilley. Kingfisher Books, New York.

Moving Picture Bible Stories Series
With pull-tab popups. Standard Publishing, Cincinnati, Ohio.

My First Bible for Tots Series
by Kenneth Taylor. Tyndale House, Wheaton, Illinois.

Bible Stories
by Norman Vincent Peale. Franklin Watts, New York.

Pop-Up Books Series
For ages four through seven.
Moses, Noah, David and Goliath.
Chariot Books, a division of
David C. Cook, Chicago, Illinois.

Read with Me Bible 106 of the
Bible's best-loved stories, to be read
aloud by, to, or with children ages
four through eight.

*Doubleday's Illustrated Children's
Bible* by Stendol Stoddard.
Doubleday, New York.

*The Storyteller's Companion to the
Bible* vol. 1, Genesis; vol. 2, Exodus–
Joshua; vol. 3, Judges–Kings; vol. 4,
Old Testament Women; and vol. 5,
Old Testament Wisdom.

Bible Treasures Series
by Ken Taylor. A Boy Helps
Jesus,The Good Neighbor, Noah
Builds a Boat, and A Very Special
Baby. Tyndale House,
Wheaton, Illinois.

My First Bible Stories in Pictures
by Ken Taylor. Tyndale House,
Wheaton, Illinois.

The Story of Creation
A picture surprise book.
Tyndale House, Wheaton, Illinois.

The Bible: Its Story for Children
by Walter Wangerin, Jr.
Rand McNally,
Chicago, Illinois.

Children's Bible Classics Series
by Bill Yenne. Easy-to-read
copy and comic illustrations.
Thomas Nelson,
Nashville, Tennessee.

Bible studies for kids

*The Book of Genesis, an Inductive
Bible Study Just For Kids*
Precept Ministries,
Chattanooga, Tennessee.

A Walk with Jesus
by Kathleen Buehler. Warner
Press, Anderson, Indiana.
A Walk with Peter and Paul
by Kathleen Buehler.
Warner Press,
Anderson, Indiana.

*Daniels for the 1990s: "We'll
Burn Before We Bend"*
Precept Ministries,
Chattanooga, Tennessee.

*The Gospel of John,
an Inductive Bible Study Just For
Kids.* Precept Ministries,
Chattanooga, Tennessee.

High Chair Devotions Series
Designed to introduce your
toddler to the Bible. Charity
Books, a division of David C.
Cook, Chicago, Illinois.

Kid Power Series
by Debbie Kennedy. Strength
Through Christ, Conquerors
for Christ, Dynamite Disciples,
Prescription for Life, and
Power Pack. Powerhouse
Publications, Atlanta, Georgia.

*Someday...A Marriage Without
Regrets* Precept Ministries,
Chattanooga, Tennessee.

and groups for parents

Women's Aglow Fellowship
InternationalP.O. Box 1548
Lynnwood, CA   98046
800-755-2456

Bible Study Fellowship
International
19001 Blanco Road
San Antonio, TX   78258
210-492-4676

Christian Women's Club
Stonecroft Ministries
P.O.Box 9609
Kansas City, MO
64134-0609

Joy of Living Bible Studies, Inc.
Doris Greig
P.O. Box 1377
Oak View, CA   93022
800-999-2703

Marilyn Hickey Ministries
8081 E. Orchard Road
Greenwood Village, CO
80111
800-743-1324

Moms in Touch International
Fern Nichols
P.O. Box 1120
Poway, CA 92074
800-949-MOMS

Moms of Preschoolers (MOPS)
Elisa Morgan
1311 S. Clarkson St.
Denver, CO   80210

Neighborhood Bible Studies, Inc.
Shirley Jacobs
34 Main St.
Dobbs Ferry, NY   10522
800-369-0307

Precept Ministries
Kay Arthur
P.O. Box 182218
Chattanooga, TN   37422
615-892-6814

Women Today International
Vonette Bright
Campus Crusade for Christ
100 Sunport Lane
Orlando, FL   32809
407-826-2116

Way to Win—Lynn Hill
Christian Weight Support Groups
Box 774
Bear, DE   19701
800-642-8446

Wilson Family Living, Inc.
Evie Wilson
1774 N. Glassell St.
Orange, CA   92665
714-637-7900

The Women's Ministries Institute
Pat Clary
11120 Oro Vista Ave.
Sunland, CA   91040
818-352-1488

Bible Clubs and Bible Memory Organizations for Kids

Kids for Christ International
1212 Josey Lane, Suite 375
Carrollton, TX   75006
314-456-8444
This organization ministers to the entire family and churches of all denominations through:
Family Evangelistic Crusades
Bible Bowl-Church & TV
Summer Champions Week
Bible Bee USA Contests

AWANA Clubs International
1 East Bode Road
Streamwood, IL   60107
708-213-2000

Navigators
P.O. Box 6000
Colorado Springs, CO 89934
719-598-1212

Child Evangelism Fellowship
Good News Clubs
P.O. Box 348
Warrenton, MO   63383
314-456-4321

Pursuing Intimacy with Your God—conference series
Precept Ministries
P.O. Box 182218
Chattanooga, TN   37422
615-892-6814

Summit Ministries—
The summer Christian leadership seminar
P.O. Box 207
Manitou Springs, CO   80829
719-685-9103

Walk Through the Bible Seminars
61 Perimeter Park, N.E.
P.O. Box 80587
Atlanta, GA   30366
404-451-9300

The Bible League
16801 Van Dam Road
S. Holland, IL   60120
708-331-2094

Christian Bible camps for families and kids

The following is only a partial list of the many exciting, high-quality Christian camps ready to serve your family year around.

and Christian sports camps

North:

Camp Forest Springs
N8890 Forest Lane
Westboro, WI 54490
715-427-5241

Camp Shamineau
Rt. 1
Motley, MN 56466
218-575-2240

Cedar Campus
Box 425
Cedarville, MI 49719
906-484-2294

Gull Lake Bible Conference
1988 Midlake Drive
Hickory Corners, MI 49060
616-671-5155

Honey Rock Camp
8660 Honey Rock Road
Three Lakes, WI 54562
708-752-5124

Maranatha Bible Conference Center
4759 Lake Harbor Road
Muskegon, MI 49441

Michindoh
4545 E. Bacon Road
Hillsdale, MI 49242
517-523-3616

Timber-lee Christian Center
N. 8705 Scout Road
E. Troy, WI 53120
414-642-7345

East:

Brookwoods/Deer Run
Chestnut Cove Road
Alton, NH 03809
518-548-4311

Camp of the Woods
Speculator, NY 12164
518-548-4311

Camp Shenandoah Springs
HC-6 Box 122
Madison, VA 22727
703-923-4300

Sandy Cove Bible Conference
P.O. Box B
North East, MD 21901
410-287-3400

Spruce Lake Retreat
RR 1, Box 605
Canadensis, PA 18325
717-595-7505

South:

Camp of the Rising Son
French Camp, MS 39745
601-547-6169

Don Eddy Basketball Camps
4522 Black Hickory Woods
San Antonio, TX 78249
800-554-3115

Glorieta Baptist Conference
P.O. Box 8
Glorieta, NM 87535
505-757-6161

Boot Camp—annual summer camp for teens
Precept Ministries
P.O. Box 182218
Chattanooga, TN 37422
615-892-6814

Jan-Kay Ranch
Rt. 1 Box 21
Detroit, TX   75436
903-561-0231

Pine Cove Conference Center
Rt. 8, Box 443
Tyler, TX   75703
903-561-0231

Sky Ranch, Inc.
Rt. 1 Box 60-SR
Van, TX   75790
903-569-3482

T Bar M Christian Sports Camp
Box 310600
New Braunfels, TX   78131
512-625-2164

West:

Camp SAMBICA
4114 W. Lake Sammamish
Pkwy S.E.
Bellevue, WA   98008
206-746-9110

Cannon Beach Conference Center
289 N. Spruce
Cannon Beach, CA   97110
503-436-1501

The First Bible & Missionary
Conference Center
4605 Cable St.
Bellingham, WA   98226
206-733-6840

Forest Home Christian Conference
Center
Forest Falls, CA   92339
909-794-1127

Hume Lake Christian Camps
256 N. Maple
Fresno, CA   93702
209-251-6043

Mount Hermon Association, Inc.
Box 413
Mount Herman, CA
408-335-4466

Royal Family Kids Camps
(for abused children)
Wayne & Diane Tesch
1968 Salinas Avenue
Costa Mesa, CA   92626
714-556-1420

Mid-America:

Camp Id-Ra-Ha-Je
591 County Rd 43
Baily, CO   80421
303-674-8442

Eagle Lake Camp
Box 6000
Colorado Springs, CO   80934
719-472-1260

Focus on the Family Basketball
Camp Ministry
8605 Explorer Drive
Colorado Springs, CO 80920
719-531-3370

Young Life's Frontier Ranch
Box 2025
Buena Vista, CO   81211
719-395-4111

Kanakuk Kanakomo Kamp
1353 Lakeshore Drive
Branson, MO   65616
417-334-2432

Maranatha Bible Camp
& Conference Center
HC 01, Box 51
N. Platt, NE   69151
308-582-4513

Nebraska Youth Leadership
Development Center
1609 E. Hwy 34
Aurora, NE   68818-9601
402-694-3934

YMCA Camp of the Rockies
2515 Tunnel Road
Estes Park, CO   80511
303-586-3341

For more information:
Christian Camping International
publishes a Christian Camp and
Conferenece Center GUIDE PAK
with detailed information on its
eight hundred member camps
throughout the United States.

Write or call:
Christian Camping International
Box 62189
Colorado Springs, CO
80962-2189
719-260-9400

Let's Hide the Word !